FLOWERS
FOR CAKES

FLOWERS
FOR CAKES

ALISON PROCTER

MEREHURST

ACKNOWLEDGEMENTS

I should like to thank my husband Tony and my family for all their support; Mary Warren, who first gave me the idea of decorating cakes; Pat and Hadyn Durant who persuaded me to do my first celebration cake; Squires Kitchen, Farnham, Surrey; Joan Mooney — leaf moulds. Pettinice used in decorating the cakes depicted in this book provided by courtesy of Bakels.

In view of the recent publicity in the United Kingdom over the small risk of salmonella in raw eggs, you may prefer to use gum arabic solution instead of egg white for making the flowers in this book. A recipe for gum arabic solution is given on page 110. Likewise, pure albumen powder can be used to make royal icing. Instead of each egg white, mix 1 teaspoon pure albumen powder with 3 teaspoons water and leave to soak in a screw-top jar, shaking occasionally. Leave to stand for 24 hours, then strain before use. Keep in the fridge.

A standard spoon measurement is used in all recipes.
1 teaspoon = one 5 ml spoon
All spoon measures are level.

Ovens should be preheated to the specified temperature.

Eggs used in the recipes are standard size (ie. size 3) unless otherwise stated.

For all recipes, quantities are given in metric, imperial and cups. Follow one set of measures but not a mixture as they are not interchangeable.

In England, cocktail sticks are made of wood and are pointed at both ends. To make a blunt end, cut off one pointed end and round off the cut end. In the United States, toothpicks are made of bamboo and are pointed at one end and carved at the other end. To make a blunt end, cut off the carved end and smooth until round with fine sandpaper or an emery board.

Published 1991 by Merehurst Limited
Ferry House
51-57 Lacy Road
Putney
London SW15 1PR

© Marshall Cavendish Ltd, 1991
Reprinted in 1994

A catalogue record of this book is available from the British Library

ISBN 1-85391-432-0

Editor: Felicity Jackson
Designer: Julie Staniland
Photographer: Michael Michaels
Illustrator: Simon Roulston
Production: Craig Chubb
Typeset by ABM Typographics Limited, Hull

Colour separation by Scantrans Pte Ltd, Singapore
Printed in Hong Kong

CONTENTS

INTRODUCTION

Nature is an everchanging beauty which many of us love to enjoy and explore. This delightful book demonstrates how, with a little patience and careful observation, it is possible to recreate the most life-like flowers out of sugar.

The book is an A-Z guide to making different flowers, explaining in detail how to make every part of the flower and then how to carefully shade and colour the petals, so that you can create exquisite flower arrangements which may be used to decorate cakes for all occasions.

The flowers may at first glance seem quite complicated, but you will find once you break them down into their component parts they become a much less daunting task to undertake and many are, in fact, relatively simple.

Cake decorating has now become a craft that is worldwide, each nation making its own impact while constantly learning from others. The delightful part of it is that it can be taken to whatever the level of each person's ability. It is very much a shared art form, in that the cake being decorated may be specifically designed for one person but it will delight many.

Perhaps flower making is an escape into fantasy world, but it is surprising how much you can learn about plants around you, possibly noticing things for the first time in your life.

When creating flower cakes, it is especially important to observe nature in the wild. Go out for walks and note how the seasons change. Watch the effect of sunlight on flowers, look at leaves freshened by a shower of rain.

You don't always have to achieve botanical perfection, it is often more a matter of trying to capture the character of the plant, and this is perhaps the magic which supercedes various techniques, knowledge of botany, or formal art or floristry training. From this, it can be seen that it is quite possible for anyone to gain immense enjoyment from an act of creation they probably didn't realise they were capable of achieving.

For the more adventurous, painting straight onto the surface of the cake with vegetable colourings can extend the horizons of the design; the more timid should try painting on plaques in case of mistakes.

Sometimes the concept of the design will come from having the fresh flowers, or a good picture, in front of you. It is very difficult to think up original work, and this book aims to give you lots of fresh and exciting ideas, then you can experiment, mixing and matching flowers to make your own personal design on your cakes.

BASIC EQUIPMENT

Flower paste (see page 111) for modelling the flowers, fine wire in different sizes, rolling pin and board, assortment of modelling tools, petal cutters, good variety of colourings (see opposite), egg white or gum arabic, paintbrushes in different sizes, florists' stretch tape for wrapping around stems, small sharp scissors, tweezers, sponge foam, such as the type used as pan cleaners, polystyrene blocks, cocktail sticks (toothpicks), wood dowling, cornflour (cornstarch), plain piping tubes (nozzles), cake boards, ribbons.

Equipment and Basic Flower making methods

There are three basic methods of making most flowers and by using one or other of these, or sometimes a combination of two or more, you will be able to create all the flowers shown in this book. If you are not sure about all the different parts of a flower, such as the stamens, pistil and calyx, see the diagram on page 10.

Nature is never dull and within any one plant there are many shadings and gradations of colour. In contrast any paste made from sugar looks totally flat, so you need to use your imagination and blend different colours and tones into leaves, and vary the shadings of the petals of a flower to make them look more natural.

Straight lines are rarely seen in nature, so curve petals and allow stems to trail and bend. Look at the growing plant and see how it holds its flower heads, the arrangement of its leaves and the colour of its stem and try to copy these as much as possible. Note the arrangement of the veins on a leaf and its edges.

The basic equipment needed for making flowers is listed on the opposite page and, as these items are needed for all the flowers in the book, the entire list is not repeated for each individual flower instruction. However, the colour of paste, size of wire, colourings and dusting powders and any specific equipment required for making a particular flower is given with the instructions for that flower.

The individual flower instructions each illustrate the petal cutter needed to make that flower, or refer you to the cutter used for one of the other flowers. If you do not have that particular cutter, you can use the illustration as a template; simply trace it on to a piece of lightweight cardboard, cut out the shape and place it on your paste, then cut out with the tip of a sharp knife or small scissors. A few of the flowers do not require a cutter at all.

You need to have a good supply of cocktail sticks (toothpicks) ready before you start on any flower, as paste will collect on the sticks (toothpicks) and once it has dried it may tear the delicate sugar petals while they are being worked. Always cut off one end of the stick (toothpick) and then smooth it with an emery board until rounded. Leave the other end sharp.

COLOURINGS

These are available in various forms and are used in slightly different ways. The paste colours, concentrated liquids and dusting powders are available from specialist cake shops.

Paste colours

These are little pots of colour which are used for colouring the paste before making the flower; they are not used for painting the finished flowers. To use, simply ladle out a little on the end of a cocktail stick (toothpick) onto a lump of paste, then knead in.

Concentrated liquids

These can be used both for colouring the paste and painting the flowers. To use, tip a few drops straight from the bottle onto the paste. If you want to mix colours to colour the paste a certain shade, you can still tip it out drop by drop onto the paste, you don't need to mix it first. However, if you are painting directly onto flowers, mix the colours first and then paint on with a fine paintbrush (preferably sable).

Dusting powders

These are good both for highlighting and for when you want more subtle, softer colours. They are also easy to use when you want a tiny amount of colour such as for the centre of a flower. They are generally used dry and painted on.

Food colourings

These are the bottled colourings available in supermarkets and food stores. They are only suitable for painting on the flowers, not for colouring the paste as they alter the consistency of the paste. They are cheaper than the other colourings but you don't get the range of colours that you get with the other colourings.

ARRANGING THE FLOWERS

All the flowers and leaves shown in the book are made on thin wire, and when they are displayed on celebration cakes, great care must always be taken to make sure there is no possibility of the wire being eaten with the cake.

All the flowers shown on top of the cakes in this book are arranged in a small plastic container with a pointed end, which is filled with flower paste. The flowers are arranged in the container, then the container is pushed into the cake so it is level with the surface of the cake.

When the cake is cut, the flowers and container can be taken out of the cake and kept as a keepsake – this way there is no danger of any of the wires coming into contact with the cake and the flower arrangement itself does not have to be disturbed in order to eat the cake. The plastic container can be put into a stand so that it can be displayed on a mantlepiece, table or shelf.

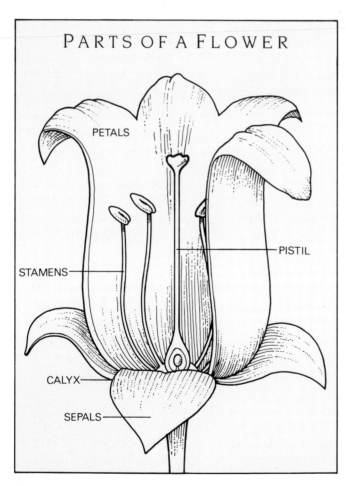

PARTS OF A FLOWER

PETALS

PISTIL

STAMENS

CALYX

SEPALS

If you are unsure about the various parts of a flower mentioned in the instructions in this book, the diagram above shows you where they are.

MAKING FLOWERS

Work with a small amount of paste at a time and keep the remainder covered to prevent it drying out and hardening. In most cases, you will need to colour the paste before making the flower, but certain flowers are coloured after they are made (see the individual flower instructions).

Always work the paste slightly, until it is pliable and stretchy, before rolling out. Don't roll it out too thinly – instead work on the edges to give the impression of all-over delicacy. When cutting out petals, try to cut a few extra ones in case of breakages. To avoid a flower being damaged while it is being made, place it on a small piece of polystyrene, during the various stages and while it is drying, then transfer it to a larger piece when it is finished.

Old paste, as long as it is still workable, can be used for the centre of flowers like chrysanthemum, cyclamen or rose, where it will be covered by petals.

The three basic flower methods are pulled flowers, Mexican hat method and paste rolled flat and cut with cutters.

Pulled flowers

For this method you will need a piece of wood dowling which has been sharpened like a pencil, but rounded off instead of pointed. Break off a small piece of paste, roll it into a ball, then form it into a cone shape. Push the blunt end of the cone onto the piece of wood dowling. Cuts can then be made around the cone according to the number of petals required. The petals can then be worked on either by squeezing between the fingers or by rolling with a cocktail stick (toothpick).

Mexican hat method

This gets its name from the shape the paste is formed into on the board before a cutter is used. Form a small piece of paste into a cone as for pulled flowers (above), then roll out the paste round the edge, leaving a centre column. Place the cutter over the column and press into the paste to cut the shape you require.

Flowers made with cutters

This is the simplest method of the three. Roll out the paste thinly on a board and then use the required cutter for that particular flower to produce the shapes of the petals.

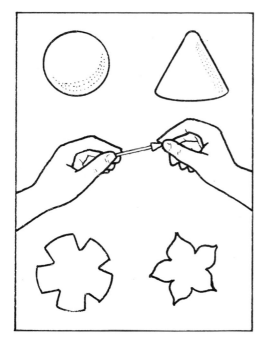 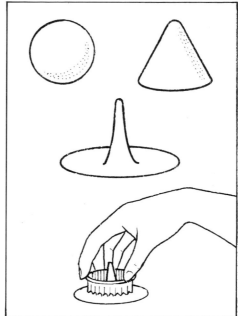

*Pulled flowers (left): form piece of paste into a cone. Push blunt end onto wood dowling. Cuts can then be made around cone according to number of petals required. **Mexican hat method:** form paste cone, then roll out edge, leaving a central column. Place cutter over column and press to cut.*

Cupping petals

To cup petals, use a balling tool to put pressure on each petal while the flower is on a piece of foam; this will then very gently curve the petals into a more life-like shape.

Working the edges

No paste should just be left after it has been cut; always either ball the edge, i.e. press it with a balling tool, or roll it with a cocktail stick (toothpick), bearing in mind the graining of the leaf or petal you are making. To ball the edge of the petal, use a large or small balling tool depending on the size of the flower. Hold the ball end of the tool half on and half off the edges of the petal and carefully thin down the edges of the paste.

Buds and leaves

Use plenty of buds, which are usually quick and easy to make, and leaves. Try to vary the size and colour. Remember that nature usually reflects surrounding colours – flower paste as flowers remains 'dull', so use your imagination and always try to add an extra dimension with different colours. With leaves, take note of which ones have a shiny upper surface and always try to add colour tones with powder or liquid colourings.

HANDY TIPS

■ When making flowers for an arrangement on a cake, make several flowers at the same time, so that you have them at different stages and work on one while another one is drying.

■ Always knead the paste before you roll it out, even if it feels soft.

■ When using cutters, if you think you are getting a furry edge to the petal, wipe the cutter with the paste still inside it on the palm of your hand.

■ Use tweezers for all the very dainty work like pushing stamens into the centre of the flower and bending the wire of the finished flower.

■ You may need cornflour (cornstarch) on your modelling tool so that it doesn't stick especially if the paste has been on the board and then turned over.

■ Work with absorbent paper beside you when you are painting flowers, so that you can dab the brush on it and the paper will absorb the excess liquid – if you put too much liquid on the flower paste the petals may dissolve.

■ Cover paste with plastic wrap when not using to prevent it drying out.

A - Z OF FLOWERS

Alstroemeria

As the subtle shading and lines are very important characteristics of this plant, it is a good idea to buy a spray of the flowers so you can copy the many different colourings on the inner and outer petals and the back of the flower.

YOU WILL NEED

30 and 28 gauge white wire and 28 and 24 gauge green wire

Different coloured dusting powders (depending on your choice of flower colour)

Greenish-brown flower paste, green flower paste plus paste of your choice of flower colour

White tape (optional)

Cutters as shown

1 Cut seven 5 cm (2 in) lengths of 30 gauge white wire. Tip dusting powder of the required colour onto absorbent kitchen paper and roll the wire in the colour. Put a tiny amount of greenish-brown paste on the end of each of six wires to make the stamens. Keep one for the pistil.

2 If you want a pistil that has separated into three at the end, cut a 7.5 cm (3 in) length of white tape and make three 1 cm (½ in) cuts at one end. Twist and roll each of these and colour to match the stamens. Roll the uncut part of the tape onto the remaining wire, then curl the three ends round and trim off to the length required (see Making a pistil).

3 Tape the stamens and pistil onto a 10 cm (4 in) length of 24 gauge green wire. When the pistil has reached this separated stage of its development it should be placed above the stamens.

4 To make the narrow, inner petals, cut three 10 cm (4 in) lengths of 28 gauge white wire. Break off a small amount of the paste of your choice and roll it into a sausage shape. Dip the end of one of the wires into egg white and pull it through the paste until about 1 cm (½ in) of wire is still embedded in the sausage shape.

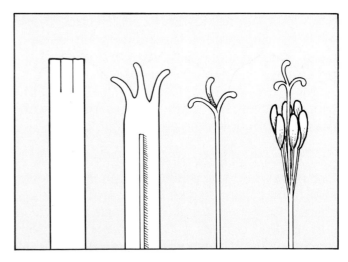

Making a pistil: make three cuts at one end of piece of tape, twist and roll, then colour to match stamens. Roll uncut tape onto remaining wire, then curl three ends round and trim. Tape pistil and stamens onto green wire.

5 Roll out the paste thinly either side of the wire and cut out a petal shape using the narrow cutter. Thin down the paste with a cocktail stick (toothpick) until wafer thin, especially on the edges. Shape the end with either scissors or a knife. Pinch the point with tweezers, and mark down through the petal with a veining tool. Make two more narrow petals in the same way.

6 These petals are sometimes curled inwards down the edge; place a cocktail stick (toothpick) on the petal and roll it towards edge, then back again, increasing pressure so paste will curl round the stick (see Curling the inner petals).

7 Make three wide, outer petals in the same way, using the larger cutter, and shape the ends with scissors. Allow the petals to dry.

8 Carefully copy the colours, noting the burgundy/brown short strokes on the narrow petals and the colouring on the backs of the flowers. Dust the colours onto the petals, noting whether the inner petals have yellow on them.

9 Take two narrow petals and place them on one side of the stamens and pistil, then put the remaining one opposite. Position the three large petals behind in the spaces in between (see Assembling the flower). Tape the stamens and petals together.

10 Take a small ball of green paste, form it into an oval shape and slightly hollow out the broader end. Paint the hollowed part with egg white and slide it up the wire and fix in position behind the petals. Roll the edge of the green paste with a cocktail stick (toothpick) to thin it down and blend it into the back of the petals. Using tweezers, pinch the green paste down its length to form ridges. Gently bend the stamens near the ends so they curve towards the two inner petals.

11 To make the leaves, form some green paste into a sausage shape. Cut a 5 cm (2 in) length of 28 gauge green wire and dip it in egg white. Pull the wire through the paste and roll out in the same way as for the petals. Cut out the long, narrow shape with scissors. Place the leaf on the palm of your hand and soften and thin down the edges with a balling tool. You may need to cut and reshape a couple of times.

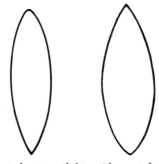

Narrow petal cutter (left); wider petal cutter (right)

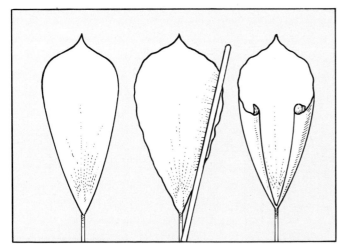

Curling the inner petals: place a cocktail stick (toothpick) on the petal just off centre and carefully roll it towards the edge of the petal, then roll back again, increasing the pressure so the paste will curl round the stick.

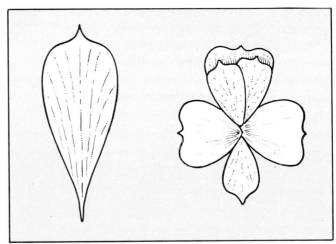

Colouring and assembling flower: when colouring, note burgundy/brown short strokes on the narrow petals. To assemble, take two narrow petals and place on one side of stamens; put third one opposite. Position large petals behind.

Anemone

*Make the petals with white flower paste and brush
on the colour when they are dry, as some flowers
have a white base to the petals and you can only
achieve this by colouring after it has been made.
The number of petals varies.*

YOU WILL NEED

Black thread
30, 28 and 24 gauge green wire
White and pale green flower colour
Cutters as shown
Yellow and yellow brown dusting powder plus colours of
your choice for the flowers
Green tape

1 Make the stamens first by winding black thread
many times round something like a pencil. Cut a
7.5 cm (3 in) length of 30 gauge wire, slide it
through this loop, then slip the loop off the pencil and twist the wire to secure the thread. Tie a
piece of the thread in a knot just above the wire
(see Making the stamens), then cut the threads.
Tape the 30 gauge wire to a 10 cm (4 in) length of
24 gauge wire. Put some tape round the base of
the stamens (the bump part).

2 Roll out some white paste thinly and cut out
one shape 'A'. Holding the shape in your hand,
soften the edge with a balling tool, then place the
shape on the board and roll it with a cocktail stick
(toothpick). Lift the petals either side of the one
on which you are working so that the petal can
really spread out. Place the flower on a piece of
foam and apply pressure with the balling tool on
each petal in turn in order to cup the edges of the
petals.

3 Paint a little egg white onto the base of the
stamens, and then slide the petals up the wire so
the stamens are in the centre. This blossom
shape may not stay in place until the second
shape is fixed into position.

4 To make the second layer of petals, roll out the
paste using the Mexican hat method (see page
10), leaving the centre column very small i.e. just
a very small bump in the middle. Cut out the
shape 'A' again, making sure the column is in the
middle. Then, working with the blunt end of a
cocktail stick (toothpick), first lengthen the petals slightly, and then thin down the edges, working from the centre to the outer edges to make it
slightly frilly. It doesn't matter if the edge is
slightly broken as it will pick up the colour better.
Turn the shape over and put on a piece of foam,
then press with the balling tool just on the edge
of each petal to cup it.

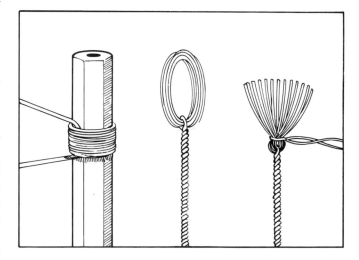

Making the stamens: *wind black thread many times round a
pencil. Slide a length of 30 gauge wire through the loop, slip
loop off pencil and twist wire. Tie a piece of the thread in a knot
just above the wire, then cut threads.*

5 Paint egg white onto the centre of the blossom shape and slide it up the wire into position behind the first petals. Pinch the small bump into the wire in order to secure the petals. With the blunt end of the cocktail stick (toothpick), press the first layer of petals down onto the second layer, so that the petals are kept at the base of the stamens. Allow to dry, then brush with dusting powder to colour them.

6 Make two leaves for each flower. Roll out some pale green paste thinly and cut out shape 'B'. Holding it on your palm, thin the edges with the balling tool. With scissors, or a knife, make cuts of different lengths in the leaf in the direction shown (see Making the leaves). Separate and roll each of the 'fingers' with the pointed end of a cocktail stick (toothpick) to thin it down; if the paste has spread, cut again.

7 Cut a 5 cm (2 in) length of 28 gauge wire, dip it in egg white and push into base of leaf. Push the leaf fronds in different directions, then allow the leaf to dry.

8 When dry, brush the edges with yellow and yellow brown dusting powder and bend the leaves so they are nearly at right angles to the wire, and place either side of the flower head. Tape the leaves into position about 1-2.5 cm (½-1 in) behind the flower.

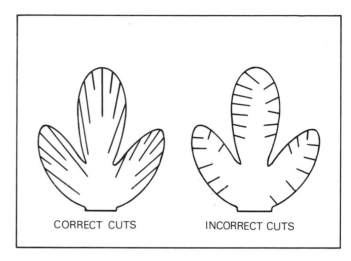

CORRECT CUTS   INCORRECT CUTS

Making the leaves: roll out pale green paste and cut out shape B. Thin edges, then make cuts of different lengths in the leaf in the direction shown. Separate and roll each of 'fingers' with the pointed end of a cocktail stick (toothpick).

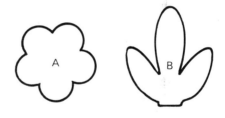

Cutter 'A' (left); cutter 'B' (right)

Making second layer of petals: roll out paste Mexican hat method, cut out shape A. With cocktail stick (toothpick), lengthen petals slightly, thin down the edges to make slightly frilly, then press from the other side to cup the petals.

Positioning the leaves: when dry, brush leaf edges with yellow and yellow/brown dusting powder and bend so they are nearly at right angles to the wire, and place either side of the flower head. Tape into position behind the flower.

Aquilegia

This wild variety of aquilegia is easier to make than the cultivated variety and the dainty flowers look pretty on a cake.

YOU WILL NEED

24 gauge green wire
Very fine white stamens
Green tape
Deep mauve or dusty pink flower paste
White vegetable fat (shortening)
Large calyx cutter as shown

1 Cut a 10 cm (4 in) length of 24 gauge wire and tape 12 stamens to the wire so that about 2 cm (¾ in) of the stamens shows above the level of the tape.

2 Take a piece of paste about the size of a small marble. With plenty of white vegetable fat (shortening) on your fingers, change the ball shape into a cone, rolling the narrow end on the palm of your hand until it is very fine.

3 Hollow out the flat end of the cone until it is very thin on the edge, then cut a section away from half the petal (see Shaping the petals).

Pinch lower edge and turn top edge back. Make six petals this way (five are needed, the extra one is in case of breakages). Keep the petals bending the same way and curl the pointed end. Place the petals on foam and leave to dry overnight.

4 The next day, mix a small piece of mauve or pink paste with egg white on a plate until it is a very creamy consistency (a bit like glue). Form another piece of paste into a band to go round the tape holding the stamens and cover this with the 'glue' (see Making a collar of paste).

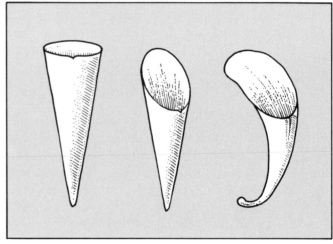

Shaping the petals: *shape some paste into a cone, rolling narrow end until very fine. Hollow out the flat end until it is very thin on the edge, then cut a section away from half the petal. Pinch top edge and turn the edge back.*

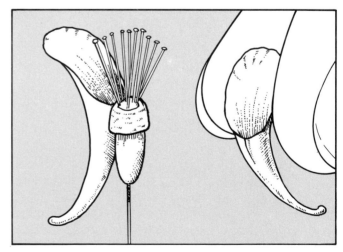

Making a collar of paste: *mix some mauve or pink paste with egg white until it is like glue. Form another piece of paste into a band to go round the tape holding the stamens to make a collar and cover this with the mauve or pink glue.*

5 Holding the wire and stamens in one hand, take the cone-shaped petals and press them into the collar. Insert the wire into a piece of polystyrene and leave to dry for a few hours. Check every so often to make sure parts have not moved.

6 Roll out some paste thinly, then cut out a calyx shape using the large calyx cutter and cut out each segment, thin the edges, then with the segments on a piece of foam indent with a dresden tool through the centre.

7 Turn over each piece of the calyx and paint egg white onto one end (see Making the calyx) and press each one into position between the spurs. Carefully balance the finished flower on top of a narrow necked bottle, such as a small medicine bottle, and leave until it is completely dry.

Bluebell

No cutter is required for this flower. Do not use too deep a blue for the paste as the flowers need to be dusted a darker colour when dry.

YOU WILL NEED

Blue and green flower paste
30 gauge white wire, 26 gauge pale green wire and 28 gauge green wire
Small, fine stamens, either yellow or white-tipped
Green and blue dusting powder
Pale green tape

---

1 Take a pea-shaped piece of blue paste and form it into a long thin cone, slightly longer than the length needed for the finished flower.

2 Open up the point of the cone with the pointed end of a cocktail stick (toothpick) and hollow out about two thirds of the length. Using small sharp scissors, cut six 'V' shapes for the petals then, holding the flower against your index finger, roll each petal with the blunt end of a cocktail stick (toothpick).

3 Put the flower on a board with the petals splayed out. Place the blunt end of a cocktail

Large calyx cutter

Making the calyx: cut out a calyx shape, then cut out each segment. Thin edges and make indentations in centre. Turn each piece over and paint egg white onto one end (see above); press this between the spurs.

stick (toothpick) on each petal in turn, roll lightly towards the end, and then roll back up the petal, slightly increasing the pressure so that the edge of the petal curls back.

4 Cut a 10 cm (4 in) length of the 30 gauge white wire and make a hook at one end. Dip the hooked wire into egg white and pull it through the flower until the hook is embedded in the paste. Insert three stamens into the flower so that they show below the petals.

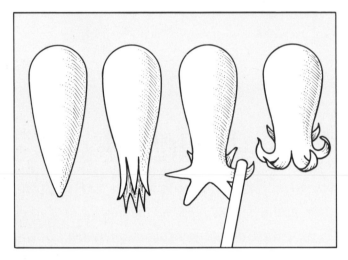

Making the petals: form a long thin cone of paste and open up the point. Cut six 'V' shapes for the petals and roll. With flower on a board, roll each petal with a cocktail stick (toothpick), rolling towards end, then back up petal.

5 Take some green paste and make some small oval-shaped buds, then make some slightly larger ones from blue paste. Fix onto lengths of white wire. When dry, dust green tips of some buds with blue and colour the stems blue by putting a little blue dusting powder on your fingers and pulling the wires through several times until the right colour is achieved.

6 Tape the buds together with pale green tape and then cut a 10 cm (4 in) length of 26 gauge pale green wire and fix on the open flowers, trying to keep them all facing the same way if the wild bluebell is wanted.

7 To make the bracts, roll out very small quantities of blue paste until very thin, then cut into very narrow strips, about 1 cm (½ in) long. Paint a little egg white on each strip and fix into place at the base of each small stem where it meets the main stalk.

8 To make the leaves, cut several 10 cm (4 in) lengths of 28 gauge green wire. Form some green paste into sausage shapes. Dip the wires in egg white and pull down through the paste until about 1 cm (½ in) is still embedded in the paste. Roll out the paste, very gently over the wire and more firmly either side until it is very thin. Cut round each wire in a leaf shape. (See page 100 for more detail on making leaves.)

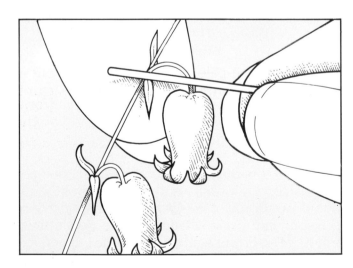

Making the bracts: roll out a small quantity of blue paste and cut into very narrow strips 1 cm (½ in) long. Paint egg white on each one and fix into place at the base of each small stem where it meets the main stalk.

Making the leaves: form some green paste into sausage shapes. Dip wires in egg white and pull down through paste. Roll out paste gently over wire and more firmly either side. Cut round each wire in a leaf shape.

Buttercup

These pretty yellow flowers look particularly good in an arrangement with daisies or, as shown on the Buttercup cake on page 80, with ivy-leaved toadflax.

YOU WILL NEED

24 gauge green wire

Fine yellow stamens

Pale green and bright yellow flower paste

Petal cutter or blossom cutter and calyx cutter as shown

Gum arabic solution (see page 110)
or confectioners' glaze

Polystyrene tray (the sort apples are sold in)

1 Cut a 10 cm (4 in) length of 24 gauge wire and make a hook at one end. Dip in egg white and fix on a small cone-shaped piece of green paste. Rough up the surface of the cone with tweezers. Cut out and curve lots of stamens and push these into the side of the cone. Allow the cone to dry before making petals.

2 If making the flower with the petal cutter, take some bright yellow paste and roll out thinly. Using the petal cutter, cut out five petals. With the petal on your hand, thin the edge of each one with a cocktail stick (toothpick), then place on a piece of foam and press with a balling tool to curve the petal slightly, taking care to keep the edge of the petal smooth. Allow to dry. When the petals are dry, paint the upper surface of each one with a little gum arabic solution or confections' glaze and set aside.

3 Roll out some pale green paste thinly, cut out a calyx using the cutter and place it in the greased polystyrene tray. Brush the dried buttercup centre with egg white below the stamens, then pull the wire through the calyx to position the stamens in centre of the calyx. Slide a paper clip over the wire behind the polystyrene tray to keep it in position.

4 Mix some yellow paste with egg white until it has the consistency of stiff royal icing. Put a little of this on the base of the petals and lay them on the calyx, one petal on each sepal. Allow to dry for 24 hours.

5 If making the flower with the blossom cutter, roll out some yellow paste and cut out the blossom shape. Cut down between each petal and thin down the edge with a cocktail stick (toothpick). Place on a piece of foam and press with a balling tool to cup the petals. Paint the centre with egg white, then pull the flower centre with the stamens pushed into the side of the cone through the petals until the flower centre is firmly in place.

6 Roll out some pale green paste and cut out a calyx. Thin down the edges, then press each of the individual sepals with a balling tool. Paint with egg white, then pull the flower on its wire through the calyx to position the calyx behind the petals. Allow the flower to dry for 24 hours.

Left to right: petal cutter, calyx cutter, blossom cutter

Carnation

This is a very easy flower to make. If you are just starting to make flowers, you may find it easier just to paint on the calyx with a pale bluish-green colour.

YOU WILL NEED

24 gauge green wire
White tape
Flower paste of your choice of colour
Two cutters as shown
Bluish-green flower paste

1 Cut a 10cm (4 in) length of 24 gauge wire. Bind some tape around one end, making a sausage shape with the tape.

2 Roll out the paste of your choice thinly and cut out two small and one large shape, using the cutters. Work on one of the small shapes first, keeping the other two well covered. Make a cut about 1 mm ($^1/_{25}$ in) into each indentation, then go round again just nicking the edge with your knife. It doesn't matter how many times you cut in each section. Roll each part well with a cocktail stick (toothpick) to frill the edge.

3 Paint the sausage shape of tape with egg white and paint a little in the centre of your first shape, then slide this shape up the wire until you reach the tape. Fold the circle of petals in half and press lightly together.

4 Squash the whole of the straight edge of the circle so that it sticks to the centre. If you do this with three fingers i.e. thumb and index finger of left hand and index finger of your right, you should avoid a square shape developing.

5 Prepare the second small shape in the same way as the first one, paint a little egg white in the centre and position it behind the first, gently pressing into place.

6 Take the large shape and cut it in exactly the same way, then put it behind the other two petals, but pull it back down the wire slightly in order to form a small bulge behind the flower. Allow to dry for a few hours.

7 To make the calyx, take a small amount of bluish-green paste, roll it into a ball, then shape into a cone. Hollow it out from the pointed end with a cocktail stick (toothpick), making the shape large enough to fit over the bulge at the back of carnation. Paint the inside of the calyx egg white, then slide it up the wire to cover the back of the flower. Trim off any excess paste.

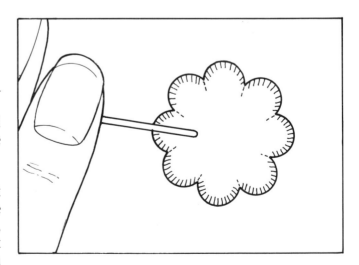

Frilling the petals: *working on one shape at a time, make a cut about 1 mm ($^1/_{25}$ in) into each indentation, then go round again just nicking all the way round the edge with your knife. Roll each part with a cocktail stick (toothpick) to frill.*

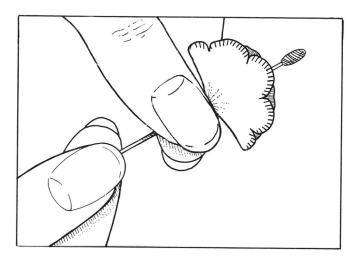

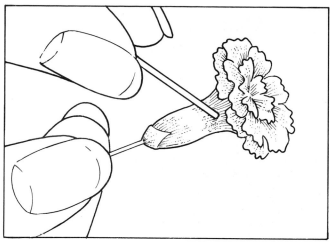

Positioning the first petal: paint the sausage shape of tape with egg white and paint a little in centre of first shape. Slide this shape up wire until you reach the tape. Fold the circle of petals in half and press lightly together.

Making a paste calyx: hollow out a cone of paste, paint inside with egg white and slide up wire to cover back of flower. With blunt cocktail stick (toothpick) held at an angle, roll paste up underneath petals, forming small points.

8 With the blunt end of a cocktail stick (toothpick) held at an angle, roll paste right underneath the petals, thus forming small points. Cut two small 'V' shapes at the base.

9 If leaves are needed for your arrangement, thinly roll out a small piece of paste. Cut out a strap shape with rounded ends about 2.5 cm (1 in) in length and 2.5 mm (⅛ in) wide and put a crease down through the middle. Paint the centre with a little egg white and slide into position, then pinch into place.

Two sizes of carnation cutter

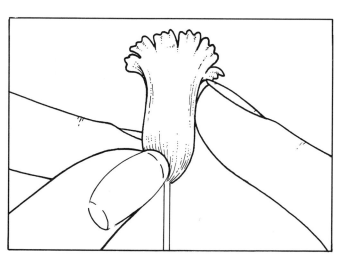

Shaping the first petal: squash the whole of the straight edge of the circle so that it sticks to the centre. If you do this with the thumb and index finger of your left hand and the index finger of your right, you should avoid a square shape.

Making leaves: roll out pieces of paste very thinly. Cut out a strap shape with rounded ends, 2.5 cm (1 in) long and 2.5 mm (⅛ in) wide. Mark a crease down the middle. Paint centre with egg white, slide it up wire; pinch into position.

Christmas rose

Christmas rose

This is just one of many different ways of making this much loved flower.

YOU WILL NEED

30, 28 and 24 gauge green wire
Cream thread
Green tape
Light green, white and green flower paste
Yellow and mauve dusting powder
Cutter as shown
Very pale green liquid colouring

1 Cut a 10cm (4 in) length of 30 gauge wire, place it alongside your finger, and wind the thread round both many times. Slide the thread off your finger, pull down the wire either side of the loop and twist tightly. Tie thread just above where the wire goes through, then cut the thread to the length required for stamens.

2 Cut a 10 cm (4 in) length of 24 gauge wire and tape the 30 gauge wire to it, then wind a little tape round the base of the thread to secure it. Separate the threads in the centre with the end of a paint brush, paint in a little egg white and drop in a tiny ball of light green paste. Holding the

threads firmly, paint ends with egg white then dip them into yellow dusting powder.

3 Place a thick piece of white paste on a board and roll out, leaving a raised part in the middle. Place the cutter over the paste and cut out the shape. Shape the petals by rolling each one with a cocktail stick from the centre (see Shaping the petals).

4 Turn the flower over, place on a piece of foam and press with a balling tool to cup petals. Brush the base of the stamens with egg white and pull the wire down through the centre of flower until the stamens sit in the paste. Allow to dry. Paint pale green at base of petals and dust underside of the petals with mauve dusting powder.

5 The leaves are an odd shape and generally have five or six sections. Make a sausage of green paste about 4 cm (1½ in) long, depending on how big you want the leaves. Cut a 10 cm (4 in) length of 28 gauge wire, dip in egg white and pull through paste. Roll out paste either side of wire and thin down. Cut to shape with scissors.

Small calyx cutter for the petals

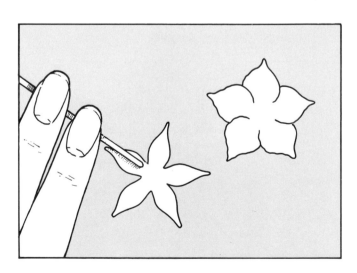

Shaping the petals: *roll each one with a cocktail stick (toothpick) from the centre (either side of the point) to change it to a rounded but pointed petal. Turn over, place on foam and press with a balling tool to cup the petals.*

Chrysanthemum

You can make these flowers in one colour only but you get a better effect using a deep colour with cream paste on the underside.

YOU WILL NEED

24 gauge green wire
Flower paste of your choice of colour plus green paste
3 sizes daisy cutters plus blossom cutter as shown
Very small balling tool such as a glass headed-pin

1 Cut a 7.5 cm (3 in) length of 24 gauge wire and make a hook at one end. Dip the hook in egg white, and cover with a small piece of paste — small enough for the petals of the smallest size daisy cutter to cover. Allow to dry.

2 Roll out the two colours of paste of your choice very thinly, then place the darker on top of the lighter paste and roll hard together until as thin as possible. No egg white is needed between.

3 Using the three daisy cutters, cut out three of the smallest size, two of the second size and three of largest size. This gives you one spare of each size in case of breakages.

4 Dip the flower centre in egg white and stand the wire in a piece of polystyrene.

5 Sprinkle board with a little cornflour (cornstarch). Work on one daisy shape at a time and keep the rest covered. Put one of the smallest flowers on the corner of the board, dark side uppermost if using two colours, and carefully but quickly cut each petal in half with a knife. As you cut, twist the blade slightly in order to separate the two halves. Using a blunt cocktail stick, (toothpick), roll each petal to wafer thickness.

6 Place the flower on a piece of foam and quickly put pressure on the ends of the petals with a small balling tool, and draw towards the centre about 2.5 mm (1/8 in). Paint middle of flower with egg white, then slide petals up wire to cover paste, but do not press petals hard onto centre.

7 Repeat for the second of the smallest daisy shapes and then for one of the medium size ones, painting egg white in centres when shaped.

8 With the first of the largest daisy shape, cut the petals only just halfway, and press some of the petals with a balling tool as above, then turn over on the foam and shape some the other way.

9 With the last daisy shape, again only cut halfway and then press all the petals on the reverse side, so that they curve downwards.

10 To make the calyx, roll out some green paste thinly and cut out a blossom shape. With the shape on the board, carefully cut a small 'V' shape from each rounded edge. Paint the centre with egg white, then pull the wire through.

Large, medium and small daisy cutters and blossom cutter

23

Clover

Although these flowers may take a little time to make you need only a few in amongst several leaves in an arrangement in order to make a dramatic impact. No cutter is required for making the flowers.

YOU WILL NEED

Pink/mauve, white, green and light brown flower paste
24 and 28 gauge green wire
Green tape
Small rose petal cutter for leaves (see page 102), optional
Green concentrated liquid colouring and gum arabic
solution mixed (see page 110)
Dark pink dusting powder

1 Take a small amount of pink/mauve paste, form into a thin sausage shape and cut at an angle into three pieces. Taking one at a time, roll the shape to a point at one end and flatten the other end. Put a blunt cocktail stick (toothpick) in the middle and bend round slightly to form a crescent shape. Make 30-40 of these pieces, but only work on three at a time or they will dry out before they are finished. Keep the size fairly small – they do not need to be all the same.

2 Make at least five open flowers. Make crescent shapes as before, but one at a time. Hollow out the flat end using the sharp end of a cocktail stick (toothpick). Thin down the rim against your index finger with the blunt end of a cocktail stick (toothpick). One side should be lower than the other. Allow the tube shape to dry before continuing with the flowers.

3 Take a tiny piece of white paste, roll it into a pear shape, then flatten and roll with a cocktail stick (toothpick) until very thin. Cut in half so that you have two tiny petals. Paint egg white inside the tube and put in the white petals facing each other (see Making open flowers).

4 Mould a fairly large piece of green paste about the size of a grape, making sure it is soft and pliable. Cut two 7.5 cm (3 in) lengths of 24 gauge green wire and tape together. Make a hook at one end. Pull this taped wire through the green paste so the hook is embedded in the paste, then pinch at the base of the paste shape to secure it. This is the flower centre.

5 Starting from near the top, make a small hole in the green paste, paint the hole with egg white, then gently push in one of the dry crescent shapes. Continue all the way down, keeping the open flowers for just over halfway down the flower centre. If any of the crescent shapes break

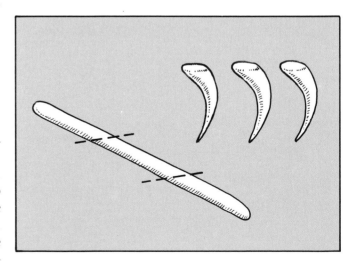

Making the small petals: make a very thin sausage of pink/mauve paste and cut at an angle. Roll each to a point at one end, flatten the other end. Put a blunt cocktail stick (toothpick) in middle and bend round to form crescent.

while you are pushing them into the green centre of the flower, don't worry as you can still use the larger parts of broken pieces.

6 It is sometimes difficult to push these petals into the lowest part. If you have difficulty, take some brown paste, roll up very small quantities and stick onto the centre with egg white – these are the dried, dead flowers, so keep them looking crumpled.

7 To make the leaves, take a marble-size piece of green paste and form into a sausage shape. Cut a 5 cm (2 in) length of 28 gauge green wire, dip one end in egg white and pull it through the green paste. Roll out the paste on either side of the wire, then either cut out the leaf shape with a small rose petal cutter, or cut out the shape with scissors. Make three for most of the leaves and four for a few of them.

8 Allow to dry, then paint the leaves with green colouring and gum arabic solution, leaving a 'V' shape of paler colour across the full width. Tape three together and occasionally four. Tape the leaves and flowers together.

9 Carefully dust the completed dry flower with a slightly darker pink dusting powder than the paste colour, keeping the dusting powder well clear of the tiny white petals.

■ In some parts of the world it is considered good luck to find a four-leaved clover as they are quite rare, so when using these flowers on a cake, put lots of the normal three-part leaves together with one or two of the four-part leaves to bring good fortune. Different types of clover have varying shapes of leaves – they can be rounded or pointed and don't necessarily have the paler 'V' shaped markings. The four-leaved clover represents 'Be Mine', the red clover 'Industry' and the white clover 'Think of me'.

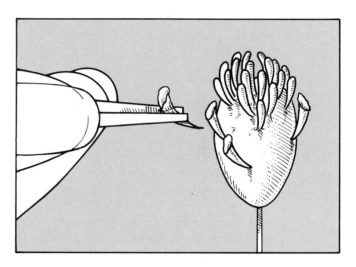

Positioning the petals: make flower centre then, starting from near the top, make a small hole in paste, paint hole with egg white, then push in one of the crescent shapes. Continue all the way down, keeping the open flowers for bottom half.

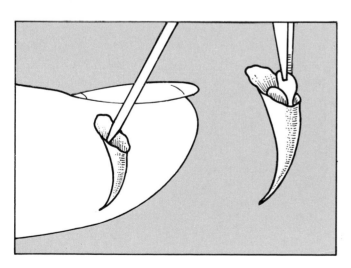

Making open flowers: make crescent shapes, hollow out the flat end using the sharp end of a cocktail stick (toothpick) and thin down rim against your index finger; one side lower than other. Make two tiny white petals and position in tube.

Making the leaves: cut out the leaf shape with a small rose petal cutter, or scissors. Allow to dry, then paint, leaving a 'V' shape of paler colour across the full width. Tape three, and sometimes four leaves, together.

Cornflower

This flower looks a bit complicated, but once you master the technique of making florets, it is well worth the effort.

YOU WILL NEED

24 gauge green wire
Green and blue flower paste
Mauve colouring
Black stamens
White dusting powder

1 Cut a 10 cm (4 in) length of 24 gauge wire and make a hook at one end.

2 Form a cone shape with a small amount of green paste. Hollow out the cone to make the calyx by putting the pointed end of the cocktail stick (toothpick) in at the narrow tip of the cone, leaving a thick part at the bottom. Thin the edge by holding it against your index finger and rolling hard with a cocktail stick (toothpick).

3 Carefully cut about six small 'V' shapes around the edge and bend the points outwards. The hollowed out centre of the calyx should measure at least 1 cm (½ in) across. Dip the wire into egg

white and pull down through the calyx until the hook is embedded in the thicker bottom part. Allow to dry overnight.

4 Make the florets one at a time. Break off a very small quantity of blue paste, roll it into a ball, then shape into a long thin cone, and flatten the broad end (you may need some white vegetable fat (shortening) on your fingers at this point). With the pointed end of a cocktail stick (toothpick), push well into the cone to open out, then, holding paste against your index finger, roll hard until the edge of the paste is very thin. Cut out as many 'V' shapes as possible, thin down the points with the blunt end of a cocktail stick (toothpick), and bend them outwards all the way round the flower.

5 Paint a little egg white on the inside of the calyx and lay each floret as it is made into position around the rim. Pull some up and some down as you arrange them.

6 Add mauve colouring to some blue paste and roll out to about 4 cm (1½ in) long and 5 mm (¼ in) wide and cut halfway down with a sharp knife, keeping the cuts very close together (see Making the flower centre). Paint the uncut edge with egg white and roll up. Separate the tasselled edge, then place in the centre of the flower, pushing well down.

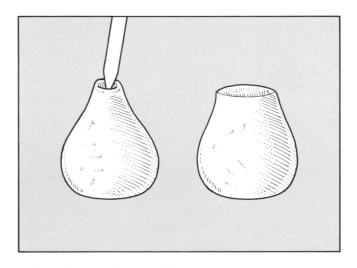

Making the cone shape for the calyx: *form a cone shape with a small amount of green paste. Hollow out the cone by putting the pointed end of the cocktail stick (toothpick) in at the narrow tip of the cone, leaving a thicker part at bottom.*

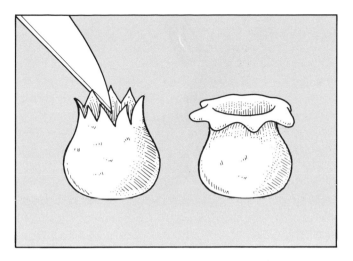

Thinning the calyx edge: hold the edge against your index finger and roll hard with a cocktail stick (toothpick). Cut about six small 'V' shapes around the edge and bend points outwards. The centre should measure at least 1 cm (1/2 in).

Making the flower centre: roll out blue/mauve paste to about 4 cm (1 1/2 in) long and 5 mm (1/4 in) wide and cut halfway down with a sharp knife, keeping cuts very close together. Paint uncut edge with egg white and roll up.

7 Cut the black stamens into short lengths, dipping some in egg white, and then into white dusting powder, and push them all well into the centre of the flower.

8 Mark the calyx carefully with a black pen, and shade each little scale shape.

■ Only attempt to make the leaves for the cornflower if you are displaying the flowers on their own, as they are single, narrow shapes which would be extremely fragile when made

from paste. If you are making cornflowers for a wedding cake, it is best to keep the number of flowers to a minimum and make lots of pretty bows from ribbon of the same shade of blue as the flowers. Keep other flowers well away from the cornflower heads if taping them into sprays, as the cornflower florets are very delicate. Poppies and daisies are the flowers most usually associated with cornflowers, but the effect of red, white and blue is a little harsh, so use cream and pale green ribbons to represent summer grasses and break up the colour masses.

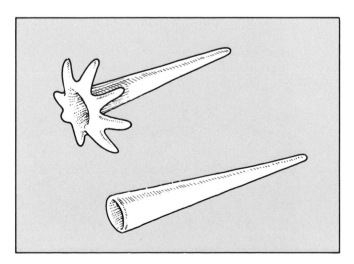

Making the florets: shape the blue paste into a long thin cone, then open up the flat end with a pointed cocktail stick (toothpick). Roll paste until edge is very thin, then cut out 'V' shapes, thin down points and bend outwards.

Finishing the calyx: when the florets and flower centre are assembled and the black stamens have been pushed into the centre of the cornflower, mark the calyx carefully with a black pen and shade each little scale shape.

Cowslip

These flowers can be found growing mostly on chalk or limestone grassland. The stalks and calyx can be both pale green.

YOU WILL NEED

26 and 24 gauge pale green wire
Yellow, pale green and dark green flower paste
Small primrose cutter as shown
Wood dowling
Pale green stamen
Orange or deep yellow concentrated liquid colouring
Pale green tape
Very small balling tool, such as glass-headed pin
Green concentrated liquid colouring and gum arabic solution mixed (see page 110)

1 Cut several 7.5 cm (3 in) lengths of 26 gauge pale green wire and make a small hook at one end of each one.

2 Take a small ball of yellow paste and make a Mexican hat shape (see page 10) on a board, keeping the central column (the throat of the flower) very slender, and the paste on the board very thin. Carefully cut out a primrose shape with the primrose cutter, making sure the central column is in the centre of the cutter.

3 Holding the flower head gently in one hand, open up the throat of the flower with the sharp end of a cocktail stick (toothpick), and lean against each petal in turn with the stick (toothpick). Thin down each petal by rolling the blunt end of the cocktail stick (toothpick) hard along edge of petals, starting from centre and rolling outwards. If you have destroyed the heart shape, re-cut with scissors.

4 Put the flower head on a piece of foam and cup each petal by applying a little pressure with the balling tool. Repeat the process to make several heads and allow to dry.

5 To make the calyx, take a small amount of pale green paste, form it into a cone, then hollow out about a third of the way down from the pointed end. Using small, sharp scissors, cut five small 'V' shapes and thin down each one with the blunt end of a cocktail stick (toothpick) to make the individual sepals. Make a sausage of green paste,

6 Place the calyx on a piece of wood dowling and pinch the complete length of the calyx with tweezers in order to form a vein that stands out in the middle of each sepal. Paint a little egg white inside the calyx, then pull the wire plus the flower

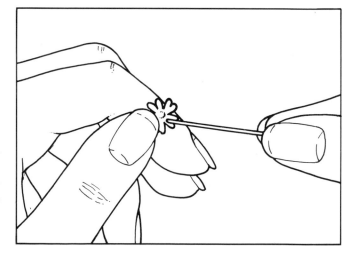

Thinning the petals: roll the blunt end of the cocktail stick (toothpick) hard along edge of each petal, starting from the centre and rolling outwards. If you have destroyed the heart shape, re-cut the shape with scissors.

down through the calyx, leaving the flower head positioned slightly above the calyx.

7 Cut off the stamen head with about a 5 mm (¼ in) length of thread, and insert it into the throat of the flower.

8 Form some calyx on their own and put on wires. On some of them close up the points of the sepals to form buds. On others leave one or two calyx with open sepals as if the dead flower has fallen away leaving just the calyx.

9 When the flowers are dry, paint a small mark of orange or deeper yellow at the base of the centre of each tiny heart-shaped petal with liquid colouring, using a fine paintbrush.

10 Holding all the heads, tape them together with pale green tape. Bend each flower stalk into a gentle curve. Add an extra 26 gauge wire for more strength.

11 Make leaves similar to those of the primrose (see page 102). Roll out some darker green paste and cut out the leaf shapes free-hand with a knife or scissors. Cut some 10 cm (4 in) lengths of 24 gauge wire, dip in egg white, then push a wire into the mid-rib of each leaf.

12 Carefully press the leaf on its wire into a prim-

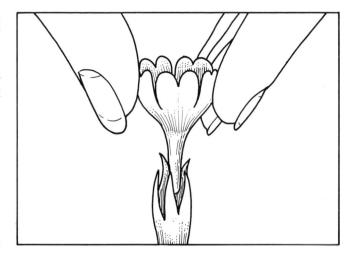

Finishing the calyx: place the calyx on a piece of wood dowling and pinch the complete length with tweezers to form a vein that stands out. Paint inside with egg white, then pull through flower on wire, leaving flower head above the calyx.

rose leaf mould to make the indentations. Turn the leaf over and carefully press a small balling tool along the edges in order to make the leaf curl slightly at the edges.

Small primrose cutter

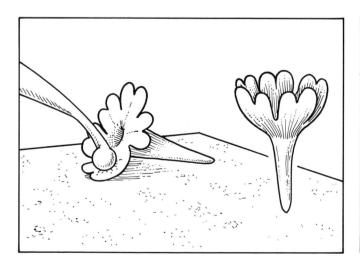

Cupping the flower head: put the flower head on a piece of foam and cup each petal in turn by applying a little pressure with the balling tool. Repeat the process to make several heads and allow to dry.

Assembling the flower: holding all the heads, tape them together with pale green tape. Bend each flower stalk into a gentle curve. Make leaves similar to those of the primrose, place tape them into position at the base of the stem.

Cyclamen

This flower has to be made in stages, preferably over a couple of days. The white or pink varieties will stay in shape better than red ones as humidity can affect the latter.

YOU WILL NEED

---

24 gauge green wire
Cutter as shown (or use part of an orchid cutter)
Plus small calyx cutter (see page 19)
White, pink or red flower paste (depending on variety you wish to make) plus green flower paste
Pink dusting powder

---

1 Cut two 15 cm (6 in) lengths of 24 gauge wire, tape together and make a hook at one end. Form a cone shape with a small amount of the white, pink or red paste.

2 Hollow out the cone with a small balling tool, but do not make the rim too thin and allow a certain depth of paste at the bottom of the cone. Dip the hooked wire in egg white and push into the cone, or pull the wire through until the hook is well embedded. Leave to dry for 24 hours before making the petals.

3 Roll out some green paste, cut out a small calyx shape using the cutter. Paint the centre with egg white and slide the calyx up the wire to cover the paste cone.

4 Place a thick piece of the paste of your choice on a board and roll out until thin. Cut out four shapes (three petals are needed, the extra one is in case of accident). Taking one petal at a time, ball the edges briefly, then work on the outside of the petal with a cocktail stick (toothpick), keeping in line with the natural veining of the petal. Start at the top and work one half, then the other half. Use a constant pressure on the cocktail stick (toothpick), rather than the frilling action used for carnations (see page 20). The effect required for this flower is a gentle curving of the petals rather than frills.

5 Firmly secure the cone shape on the wire in a piece of polystyrene. Hold the prepared petal in both hands and twist slightly. Place the narrow end of the petal over the thumb of the left hand and paint about 5 mm (¼ in) from the base with egg white.

6 Carefully place the painted narrow part into the cone and press into place with a blunt cocktail stick (toothpick). Repeat with two more petals, slightly overlapping them. If you want petals to fall in interesting positions, work on one petal at

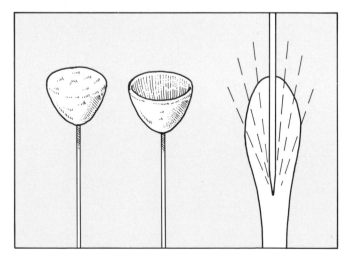

Making flowers: *hollow out cone of paste, cut out a small calyx of green paste and cover cone. Cut out three petals and ball the edges, then work on outside of each petal, starting on the top and working on one half, then the other half.*

a time on several flowers, allowing each to dry at a different angle. Leave these three petals to dry overnight before continuing with the rest of the flower.

7 The following day, bend the wire carefully, preferably using tweezers (see Shaping the flower), then turn the whole stem upside down and place the flower back in the piece of polystyrene, so the flower head is back in the original working position.

8 Roll out some more paste of the original colour and cut out two more petals for the flower. Work on the petals as before, balling the edges briefly, then working on the outside of the petal with a cocktail stick (toothpick). Gently curve the edges as before, then try and place one petal on either side of the wire, so that there is no gap round the rim apart from where the wire is. Allow these petals to dry thoroughly before continuing. Don't try to rush it!

9 Adjust the wire so it is in a gentle curve. Brush on some darker pink colour, starting from the base of petal and working up to about 5 mm (¼ in) from the base when the flowers are completely dry.

10 Cyclamen buds are pointed and when nearly ready to open the petals are twisted. You can achieve this by marking the bud with the back of a modelling knife.

11 To make the leaves, cut 5 cm (2 in) lengths of 26 gauge wire. Form some green paste into a sausage shape. Dip one of the wires in egg white and pull down through the paste until about 1 cm (½ in) is still embedded in the paste. Roll out the paste, very gently over the wire and more firmly either side until it is very thin. Cut the leaves free-hand, copying them from nature if possible. Press the edges with a balling tool to give them a feeling of movement. Take note of the colouring on the leaves of various varieties. See leaves, pages 100-103, on how to paint them. Blotches on surface of leaf can be achieved by removing paint while still wet with a cotton wool bud.

Cyclamen petal cutter

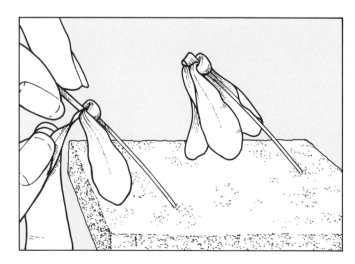

Positioning the petals: *place narrow end of petal over thumb of left hand and paint about 5 m (¼ in) from base with egg white. Place this part in cone and press into place with blunt cocktail stick (toothpick). Repeat with two more petals.*

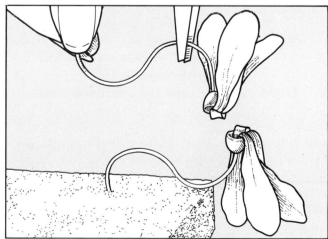

Shaping the flower: *bend the wire carefully, preferably with tweezers, then turn the whole stem upside down and place back in the polystyrene, so the flower head is back in the original working position.*

Daffodil

There are so many daffodil varieties that trumpet length and petal shape can vary enormously. Yellow powder slightly deeper in colour dusted onto the petals will help to make them look more lifelike.

YOU WILL NEED

24 gauge dark green wire
Yellow stamens
White and dark green tape
Yellow dusting powder
Yellow, green and straw-coloured flower paste

1 Cut a 10 cm (4 in) length of 24 gauge wire. Arrange six stamens around the wire, then secure them with white tape, taking care not to use too much or it will look bulky. Trim the length of the stamens to about 5 mm (¼ in). Dip them in egg white and then in yellow dusting powder to look like pollen on the stamens.

2 Roll out a small amount of yellow paste and cut out shape 'B'. Gently frill the shorter curved edge with the blunt end of a cocktail stick (toothpick).

By frilling this shorter edge a straighter trumpet is achieved. Paint a little egg white on one end, then bring round the other end to stick to it and make a trumpet shape (see Making the trumpet). Pinch the unfrilled edge so that you now have a cup shape.

3 Paint the tape holding the stamens with egg white and pull it through the trumpet so the stamens are in the centre, taking care to keep the trumpet in shape. Place the trumpet in a polystyrene block.

4 Roll out another piece of yellow paste and cut out shape 'A'. Put the shape on your hand and briefly press the edges of the petals with a balling tool then, using a cocktail stick (toothpick), work from the centre to the edge of each petal in turn to grain and thin the paste.

5 Paint a little egg white onto the back of the trumpet shape, then pull the petals up the wire and position them behind the trumpet pressing very gently to secure them.

6 Take another piece of yellow paste, roll it into a ball, then form it into a Mexican hat shape on the board (see page 10), making sure that the centre column is thin. Place the shape 'A' cutter over the centre column and cut out the shape. Lift the shape off the board and holding it over the index

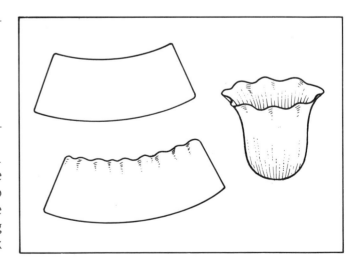

Making the trumpet: cut out shape 'B' and gently frill the shorter curved edge. Paint a little egg white on one end (shaded area), then bring round other end to stick to it and make a trumpet. Pinch unfrilled edge to make a cup shape.

finger of your left hand, roll each petal with a cocktail stick (toothpick). Open up the throat well with the cocktail stick (toothpick), paint the inside with egg white, then slide the trumpet and first set of petals down through the second set of petals. Bend some of the petals slightly to give a feeling of movement to the flower.

7 Cut another 10 cm (4 in) length of 24 gauge wire and tape it to the existing stem with green tape. Form a small oval-shaped cone of green paste, slightly hollow out one end, paint indent with egg white and slide into place directly behind the flower head. Using tweezers, bend the head.

8 Take a sausage shape of straw-coloured paste the size of a small pea and roll it out thinly, then cut into an oval shape. Using the pointed end of a cocktail stick (toothpick), mark it heavily with veins, crumple and tear slightly, then fix behind green paste using a little egg white to secure it.

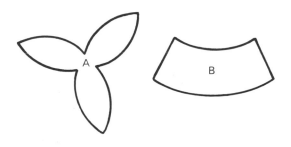

Cutter 'A' (left); cutter 'B' (right)

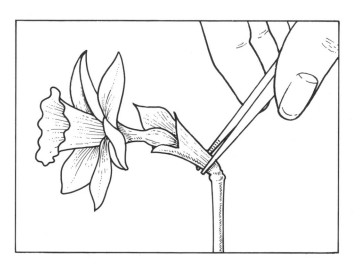

Making the calyx: *cut out an oval shape of straw-coloured paste. Using pointed end of cocktail stick (toothpick), mark heavily with veins, crumple and tear slightly, then position behind the piece of green paste using egg white to secure it.*

Daisy

The daisy makes a lovely addition to any arrangement. The leaves are best cut free-hand; make the slight indentations on the leaf edges by pressing and turning with the pointed end of a cocktail stick (toothpick).

YOU WILL NEED

24 gauge green wire
Yellow, green and white flower paste
Yellow dusting powder mixed with powdered gelatine
Red dusting powder
Cutter as shown plus small blossom cutter (see page 38)

1 Cut a 7.5 cm (3 in) length of 24 gauge wire, make a hook at one end, then turn the hook at right angles. Take a small pea-shaped piece of yellow paste and slightly flatten, dip the hook in egg white, then push it into the yellow paste so that the wire is in the centre. Allow to dry for 24 hours.

2 When the paste on the wire is dry, dip in egg white, then into the yellow dusting powder and gelatine mixture to make pollen. Stand the wire in a piece of polystyrene.

3 Take some white paste and roll it out thinly then, using the daisy cutter, cut out two shapes. Keeping one well covered, work on the other. Cut each petal in half and roll on the board with the blunt end of a cocktail stick (toothpick). Put on a piece of foam and press the ends with a very small balling tool, using slight pressure.

4 Paint the centre with egg white, then push the petals up the wire to position them behind the yellow flower centre. Repeat with the second daisy shape. Make some flowers with flat petals and some well curved towards the centre. Use a cocktail stick (toothpick) to manoeuvre the petals into life-like positions.

5 To make the calyx, roll out some green paste thinly and cut out a small blossom shape with the cutter. Press with a balling tool to thin it, then paint with egg white and push up the wire to position behind the petals. Allow to dry.

6 When dry, brush red dusting powder on underside of petals on some flowers, especially buds.

Small daisy cutter

Shaping the flowers: make some flowers with flat petals and some well curved towards the centre, using a cocktail stick (toothpick) to manoeuvre petals into interesting positions. Make buds the same way but close petals up over centre.

Freesia

The flowers are best made with white paste as the petals change colour from top to bottom, and they are best coloured after they are made.

YOU WILL NEED

24 and 28 gauge green wire
Stamen cotton (cut heads off and retain thread)
White and green tape
Single petal cutter as shown
White, green and cream flower paste
Dusting powder of your choice of colour

1 Cut a 10 cm (4 in) length of 24 gauge wire, then tape about six stamen threads to it with white tape, winding on enough tape to make a sausage shape. Hold cutter against tape and threads and trim stamens (see Trimming the stamens).

2 Separate the stamens and dip first in egg white, then in dusting powder to match the colour chosen for the finished flower.

3 Roll out some white paste thinly and, using the cutter, cut out six petal shapes. Carefully roll a cocktail stick (toothpick) from just off centre to the outer edge of each one, then repeat for the other side, leaving a slightly thicker triangle of paste at the top of each petal. Try not to thin the edge of the bottom of the petal.

4 Mark a line in the centre of each petal and one either side of the centre with a modelling tool – don't use a cocktail stick (toothpick) as this could tear the paste. Gently press the triangle of paste at the rounded end of the petal with a balling tool to curve it in and forward. Some freesias have slightly pointed petals, in which case pull out top of shape with small balling tool.

5 Paint egg white about 5 mm (¼ in) from the base of each petal upwards and stick onto the side of the tape and stamens, placing three petals round the stamens, then the remaining three in the spaces between. Hang the flower upside down to let it set. Work on three petals, allow to dry, then put on next three.

6 When the flower is dry, brush on the dusting powder of your choice, remembering that the base of the petals is often cream or yellow. Complete the colouring before making a calyx.

7 Make buds in three different colours. Make a few very small ones from green paste on 28 gauge wire, then some a bit bigger from green and cream paste mixed, and some larger still from cream paste.

8 To make a calyx, take some slightly darker green paste than that used for the small buds and form it into a cone shape. Open up the flat end with the point of a cocktail stick (toothpick), then roll round the inside with the blunt end of the cocktail stick until you have a thin hollow cone.

9 Cut out two wide 'V' shapes so that the calyx resembles a bird's open beak. Thin the cut edge with a cocktail stick (toothpick). Paint inside with egg white, then slip calyx up the wire to base of the flower. Vary the size of the calyx according to the size of the flower you are making.

10 Using tweezers, position two tiny buds next to each other, tape them together, then add any extra buds, getting larger each time until a full flower or flowers are added to complete the spray. Try to have a good look at a real spray, as the way each flower head leads from the previous one is an essential part of the character of the spray. When used in a group of flowers, use three buds together and the mature flowers alone.

Single petal cutter

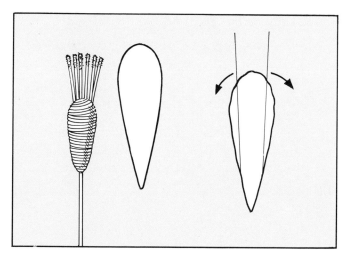

Trimming stamens and rolling petals: hold cutter against tape and threads; trim stamens just short of cutter top. Cut out petals, roll cocktail stick (toothpick) from just off centre to outer edge; leaving thicker triangle at top.

Making the calyx: form darker green paste into a hollow cone, then cut two wide 'V' shapes so that the calyx resembles a bird's open beak. Thin the cut edge. Vary size of calyx according to size of bud or flower you are making.

Fuchsia

Fuchsia stamens and pistil vary from very pale pink to darker pink, depending on the variety. They hang below the petals and are quite a feature of the flower.

YOU WILL NEED

24 gauge white wire
9 pink stamens
Green tape
Pink, red, white or mauve flower paste
Cutters as shown
Pink dusting powder

1 Cut a 10cm (4in) length of 24 gauge wire and fix nine stamens to the wire with tape; one is cut longer than the others to be the pistil. Do not use too much tape or you will have difficulty pulling the wire through the throat of the flower. Stick the wire in a piece of polystyrene.

2 Roll out some of the paste of your choice and cut out four individual petals, using the petal cutter. Press the edges with a balling tool, then place the petals on a piece of foam and place the balling tool on each petal in turn, putting slight pressure on the paste and pulling the tool from the broad end of the petal in order to curve it.

3 Paint a quarter of one petal with egg white. Repeat for the other three, arranging one on top of the other like a fan (see Making the centre petals). Paint egg white across all four petals. Take the stamens plus wire and, starting from the left hand side, use your left thumb to move the paste over the stamens and then roll until petals surround the stamens. Place the wire holding these petals in a polystyrene block while the next part of the flower is prepared.

4 Using a different colour, make a Mexican hat shape (see page 10) with a long and thin centre column. Place the other cutter over the paste, press, twist and release from the board. Open up the throat of the flower with the pointed end of a cocktail stick (toothpick), then thin the petal edges with a cocktail stick (toothpick) on the index finger of your left hand.

5 Place these petals upside down on a piece of foam then, using a balling tool, gently, but with slight pressure, bring the tool from the point of the petal towards the centre. This will make the petals turn up. Paint a little egg white in the throat, then pull the stamens and first lot of petals (called the skirt) through the centre. Brush burgundy/brown dusting powder onto stem.

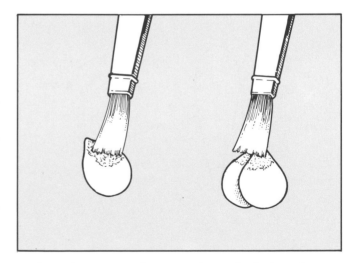

Making the centre petals: cut out four individual petals. Paint a quarter of one petal with egg white (shaded area in diagram). Repeat for other three, arranging one on top of the other like a fan. Paint egg white across all four petals.

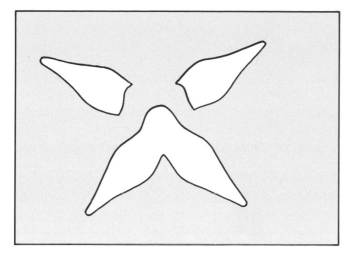

Making the decoration for the side of the fuchsia cake (see page 86): roll out some paste and cut out the shape above, using the fuchsia cutter. Ball from underneath and allow to dry. Cut out two skirt petals and allow to dry.

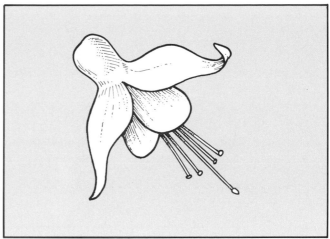

Assembling design on the side of the cake: pipe on one pistil and two stamens either side. Dust deep mauve powder onto the skirt petals and fix in place with royal icing. Fix the other petals in place with royal icing.

6 Make buds using the same colour paste as for the Mexican hat section of the flower. If making tiny buds, make them in green paste. If making leaves for your arrangement, follow the instructions on page 100.

7 Take the colouring of the stems down onto the edge of some of the leaves.

■ This well-known plant comes in a tremendous range of colours and shapes, from the small shrub-like plant which is used as a hedge, to the showpiece standards, but they all have the distinctive shape with the beautiful hanging heads. The drooping effect should always be used to advantage, never straightened out to fit in with a tight arrangement. The leaves are simple to make and should be used to set off the wonderful colourings of the flowers. Study the colour of the stems as the red pigment often follows through from the flowers down to the leaves and onto the main vein. The leaves can be arranged singly, in pairs, or in groups of three, the flowers coming from the main stem at the same point as the leaves. Many varieties have quite a gloss on the outside of the sepals, so the buds especially appear quite glossy. Confectioners' glaze or layers of gum arabic solution can achieve this.

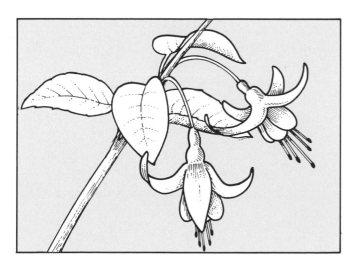

Assembling the flowers: after working the second lot of petals to make each petal turn up, paint a little egg white in the throat of the petals, then pull the stamens and first petals (skirt) through the centre.

Fuchsia cutter (left); rose petal cutter (right)

Gypsophila

This plant generally has white flowers, but there is a pink variety. Florists sometimes have the flowers dyed to fit in with colour schemes.

YOU WILL NEED

Fine rose wire
Green tape
White flower paste
Very small blossom cutter as shown
Green concentrated liquid colouring

1 Cut several 7.5 cm (3 in) lengths of rose wire and cover with tape; make a hook at one end.

2 Roll out the paste and cut out blossom shapes, using the cutter. Frill the edge of each of the tiny shapes with the blunt end of a cocktail stick (toothpick). Paint the centre of the shape with a little egg white, then pull the wire through the blossom shape and squash the shape onto the hook. Allow the first blossom shape to dry completely before placing the next one.

3 Take another blossom shape, frill as before, paint the centre with egg white and place in position behind the first. Allow to dry. Repeat to make as many flowers as you want.

4 To make buds, cut lengths of wire as for the open flowers, but do not hook them. Take tiny pieces of paste, roll into pea shapes and leave on the board. Dip the wires in egg white and push one into each piece of paste. Allow to dry.

5 When the flowers and buds are dry, paint a calyx on each flower and bud with green colouring. Tape the flowers and buds together, grouping them mainly in threes.

■ To obtain the right effect you need an enormous amount of this flower. It is usually best to tape it in groups of three, or three groups of three, otherwise it would be too big to handle alongside the other paste flowers. It must be kept dainty and as little tape as possible used to keep it together. It is best to use gypsophila mainly with cultivated flowers. When used on a cake such as the wedding cake (see page 97), vary the colour from white through to pale pastel shades.

Small blossom cutter

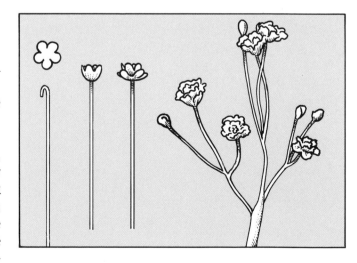

Making the flowers: *paint centre of frilled shape with egg white, then pull hooked wire through and squash the shape onto the hook. Allow to dry before placing next one. Repeat to make as many flowers as you want. Tape in groups of three.*

Hazelnuts

Hazelnuts are very quick and easy to make and look extremely effective. Where possible, copy the real thing for the correct shape.

YOU WILL NEED

24 gauge green wire
Very light brown and green flower paste
Brown dusting powder
Brown concentrated liquid colouring

1 Cut a 10 cm (4 in) length of 24 gauge wire and make a hook at one end; dip the hook in egg white. Take a piece of light brown paste and form it into the shape of a hazelnut on the end of the hooked wire. Leave to dry overnight.

2 Roll out the green paste very thinly to a strip about 5 cm (2 in) long and 1 cm (½ in) wide. Cut 'V' shapes of varying sizes along the whole length. Thin down each spike with a cocktail stick (toothpick) and trim off any points which have become rounded.

3 Paint the uncut edge with egg white and wrap it around the base of the nut, turning down some of

the points as you go. Allow the hazelnut to dry for about 30 minutes.

4 Dust the edges of the husk with soft brown dusting powder then, with a fine paint brush, paint brown liquid colouring in small amounts on the very edge.

5 Tip the nuts at an angle, so that when the wires are taped together the heads are all close together. Put any number from two to five together.

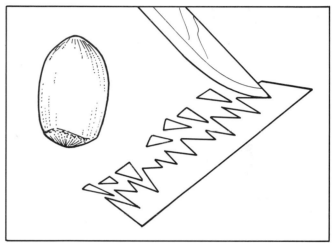

Making the nut and husk: *form some light brown paste into the shape of a hazelnut. Roll out green paste to a strip 5 cm (2 in) long and 1 cm (½ in) wide. Cut 'V' shapes along length. Thin down each spike and trim rounded points.*

Assembling the nuts and leaves: *when the dry nuts have been coloured, tip them at an angle so that when the wires are taped together the heads are all close together. You can put any number from two to five together.*

Heather

This flower is based on the Bell heather. It is easy to make but as you need a lot of flowers, it can be time consuming. No cutter is required for making the heather flowers.

YOU WILL NEED

33 gauge white wire
Pink flower paste
Olive green tape
24 gauge green wire

1 Cut several 4 cm (1½ in) lengths of 33 gauge white wire; do not hook them.

2 Take a very small piece of pink paste, form it into a cone and hollow out just the pointed end, using a cocktail stick (toothpick). Thin down the edge all the way round with the blunt end of a cocktail stick (toothpick).

3 Holding flower at the base, carefully break the edge with a cocktail stick (toothpick). Dip one of the wires in egg white and pull it through the flower. Stand the wire in a piece of polystyrene at an angle to prevent the flower slipping and allow to dry. Repeat to make as many as you want.

4 To make the leaves, cut lots of 2.5 cm (1 in) lengths of olive green tape. Cut each piece lengthways into three; feather one end of each piece and spread out the spiky leaves and roll the other end (see Making the leaves).

5 Cut a 10 cm (4 in) length of 24 gauge wire and tape flowers on in clusters with leaves in between.

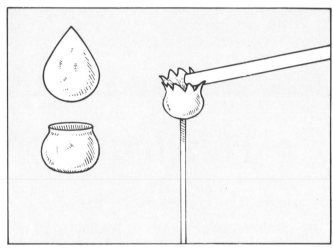

Making the flowers: form the pink paste into a cone and hollow out the pointed end with a cocktail stick (toothpick). Thin down the edge with the blunt end and then break the surface of the rim with the cocktail stick (toothpick).

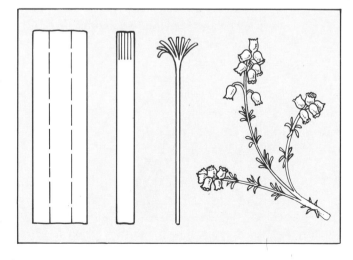

Making the leaves: cut 2.5 cm (1 in) lengths of tape and cut each piece lengthways into three. Feather one end of each piece by making small cuts and spreading out pieces; roll the other end. Tape flowers in clusters with leaves in between.

Honesty

Honesty is a very attractive plant to use in autumn arrangements, particularly with berries. It is essential that the paste is extremely thin.

YOU WILL NEED

30 or 33 gauge white wire
Very pale cream flower paste
Brown and silver dusting powder
Brown concentrated liquid colouring

1 Cut a 17.5 cm (7 in) length of 30 or 33 gauge white wire. Bend one end round two fingers, leaving piece at end, and bending wire back up to small piece being held (see Making the honesty shape). Wind wire round this and down to other side of circle, winding it in and out of circle.

2 Roll out some cream paste very thinly and place over wire. Roll paste onto wire, pressing hard, then cut away from outer edge of the wire.

3 Lift honesty off the board with a palette knife and place on foam. Holding a small balling tool at right angles to seed-head, 5 mm (¼ in) from edge, press carefully but firmly and turn to make a slight hollow. Repeat several times.

4 Make as many seed-heads as you want, then cut out areas on some to make them look weathered. Allow to dry, then paint edges with brown colouring and paint in small lines from edges to hollows with very pale brown paint. Dust with brown and silver powder. Tape together, leaving a short stem between each seed-head and main stalk.

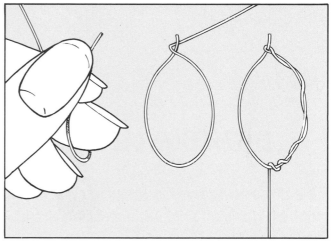

Making the honesty shape: *bend one end of wire round two fingers, leaving piece at end, and bending wire back up to small piece being held. Wind wire round this and down to other side of circle, winding it in and out of circle.*

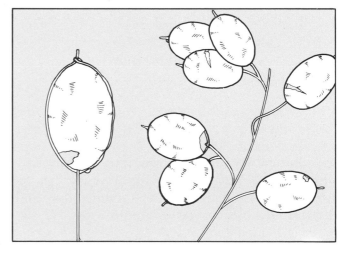

Weathering the seed-head: *cut out areas on some seed-heads to make them look weathered. Allow to dry, then paint the edges with brown colouring and paint in small lines from edges to hollows with very pale brown paint.*

Honeysuckle

There are many varieties of honeysuckle with different colours. Tiny buds are usually green, turning cream as they get larger. Watch that the largest buds are not longer than the open flowers.

YOU WILL NEED

24 and 28 gauge green wire
Cream and green flower paste
Cream thread
I white stamen with pale green tip
White and green tape

1 Cut a 10 cm (4 in) length of 28 gauge wire. Wind the cream thread round your finger so that when cut there will be five stamens. Tape these loops together with the white stamen to the wire with white tape, but do not make it too bulky. Cut the circles of thread to make the stamens, then stick the wire in a piece of polystyrene.

2 Take a large pea-sized piece of cream paste and form into a long, thin cone, pointed at one end and flat the other. Open up the flat end of the cone with the pointed end of a cocktail stick (toothpick) about halfway down and roll against your index finger to thin all around the edge of the opened up cone.

3 To form the lower single petal, make two cuts about 2.5 mm (⅛ in) apart. Roll the paste against your index finger with a cocktail stick (toothpick) until very fine. Round off the ends with scissors and curl under.

4 Cut large 'V' shapes either side of the tongue of paste so that you are left with one large petal upright and a slender one turned down (see Shaping the petals).

5 Roll the larger petal hard with a cocktail stick. Make one cut in the centre and one cut either side (three in all) about 2.5 mm (⅛ in) in depth. Round off the edges with scissors and then bend them back.

6 Open up the throat until quite hollow, paint with egg white, then pull the stamens on the wire carefully through with a twisting action. Keep working the pointed back of the flower all the time to keep it supple.

7 Working quickly, shape the flower head into an 'S' curve by pressing up with the left hand and down with the right. Roll the flower head very gently with your fingers to regain the roundness of the throat of the flower.

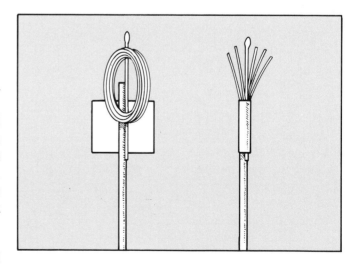

Making the stamens: wind the cream thread round your finger so that when cut there will be five stamens. Tape these loops together with the white stamen to the 28 gauge wire with white tape. Cut the circles of thread.

8 Make small buds in green paste and larger buds in cream with the same 'S' shape, but press to flatten them at the sides.

9 Taking the flower heads, and placing some of the larger buds in between, build up a circle with smaller buds more upright in the centre. Tape these all together. A bit further down the stem tape in two 10 cm (4 in) lengths of 24 gauge wire to give added length and strength.

10 Take a ball of green paste about 1 cm (½ in) in diameter and push up the wire to the flower head. With closed tweezers, push the paste up and in between the ends of the flower heads.

11 Allow to dry and then colour with a mixture of pink and brown, or a plum shade. Put some shading on the tiny buds in the centre. The more mature flowers take on a deeper yellow shade on the inside.

12 Make some heads of just the small buds and some heads of red and green berries.

■ This well-loved flower comes in many shapes, sizes and shades. The leaves are amongst the earliest in the year to start growing and so are easily found in the hedgerows and woodlands. Some varieties only have a couple of florets either side of the stem, so you don't need to make very many to give the effect of this delightful flower. If you are making a display of country flowers for a wedding cake, use the honeysuckle buds on the top tier, half open flowers on the middle cake and a fully mature head with many open florets on the bottom tier. The clusters of berries are also very useful in an arrangement as the tightly packed green and red berries go well with most colour schemes. The cream flowers can be used to advantage, especially where the other flowers in the arrangement are darker.

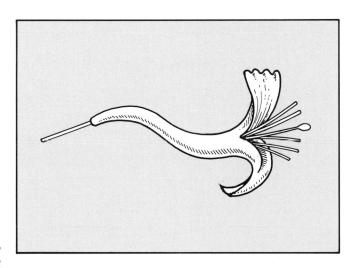

Finishing the petals: *round off edges of larger petal and bend back. Open up the throat, paint with egg white and pull stamens on the wire through. Shape the flower head into an 'S' curve by pressing up with left hand and down with the right.*

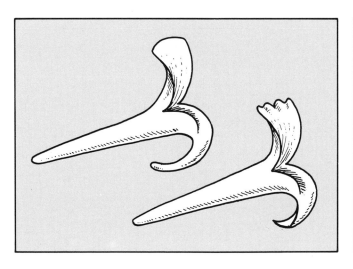

Shaping the petals: *open up cone, thin edge. Make two cuts 2.5 mm (⅛ in) apart; roll paste, round off ends and curl under. Cut 'V' shapes to make large upright petal and a slender one turned down. Roll larger petal, make three cuts.*

Assembling the flower: *take the flower heads and, placing some of the larger buds in between, build up a circle with smaller buds in the centre. Tape together. Further down the stem tape in two 10 cm (4 in) lengths of 24 gauge wire.*

Ivy-leaved toadflax

This is time-consuming to make, but it is a very pretty flower with an attractive way of trailing and this can be used to accentuate curves in a design.

YOU WILL NEED

28 gauge green wire
Pale lilac, yellow and green flower paste
Lobelia cutter as shown
Green tape

1 Cut several 7.5 cm (3 in) lengths of wire and make a hook at one end of each. Take a small pea-size piece of lilac paste and make a very small Mexican hat shape (see page 10) then, using the cutter, cut out the shape.

2 Open up the throat of the flower with the pointed end of a cocktail stick (toothpick), then thin down the petals with the blunt end, either against the side of your index finger or on the board. Push in a very small balling tool in order to form a slight hollow. Dip one of the hooked wires in egg white and pull it through the flower at an angle, so that it comes out about halfway down the throat of the flower.

3 Take a very small piece of yellow paste, small enough to fit into the throat. Press a cocktail stick (toothpick) lightly onto this paste to divide it into two sections. Paint the throat of the flower with egg white and place the yellow paste in position in the throat of the flower.

4 The calyx on this flower is extremely small and can either be made out of paste or tape. If using paste, take a tiny piece of green paste and form into a cone shape. Open up the flat end and thin down the edge with a cocktail stick (toothpick) against your finger, then cut out five 'V' shapes. Paint the inside with egg white and slide the calyx up the wire into position behind the flower. If using tape, cut off a short length, about 5 mm (¼ in), and, working from the side of the tape cut out five 'V' shapes. Roll the tape onto the wire immediately behind the flower head.

5 To make the leaves, roll out some green paste, leaving a slightly thicker part through the middle. If you have a real leaf press it into the paste and then cut round the impressions with scissors. Alternatively, choose one of the designs opposite (see Ivy-leaved toadflax leaves).

6 Cut a 5 cm (2 in) length of 28 gauge green wire, dip in egg white, then push into the thicker part of the paste leaf. Using a modelling knife, mark the veins, then allow to dry.

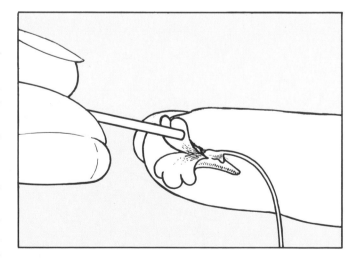

Pulling the wire through: *open up the throat of the flower, thin down the petals and form a slight hollow, then dip a hooked wire in egg white and pull it through the flower at an angle, so that it comes out about halfway down the throat.*

7 When using the leaves as a decorative edging on the side of the cake, start by picking a selection of well-shaped leaves and put them in water. Roll out some green paste and cut out a strip about 7.5 cm (3 in) long and 2.5 cm (1 in) wide. Take one leaf and press the back of it onto the paste several times along the length of the strip (about four or five times). Cut off one shape and cover the remainder to prevent them drying out. Cut out the leaf shape, mark the veins and allow to dry, then repeat with the other leaves. Fix the individual leaves onto the cake with a small amount of royal icing.

8 When taping the ivy-leaved toadflax plant together the usual arrangement is one leaf and one flower coming from the main stem of the plant at the same point.

■ Although this is a very common plant, many people are unaware of it as it grows mainly in walls, and many gardeners treat it as a weed. It originally came from the Mediterranean region and was a popular rockery plant in the 17th Century. From there it escaped to become the widespread plant it is today.

Close inspection will show you what a delightful little flower it is, with many different shapes of leaf on the one plant. You don't need to vein the leaves as they are very small. The lovely curving stems can be used in an arrangement for a de-corative cake without having to attach too many leaves and flowers.

The soft violet colouring goes particularly well with flowers like buttercups, daisies and primroses, but also looks good with honesty and thistles. To save yourself time and effort, make some tiny buds instead of full open flowers. For the calyces use tape with 'V' shapes cut out, as this gives a much daintier effect and is much quicker to make.

Even though the flowers are so small, it is still worthwhile dusting them with a slightly darker shade, making sure that the centre lobes stay a good clear yellow. There is no reason why this flower couldn't be used on a wedding cake as part of the bridal bouquet to give a wonderful trailing effect down the sides of the different tiers of the cake.

Lobelia cutter

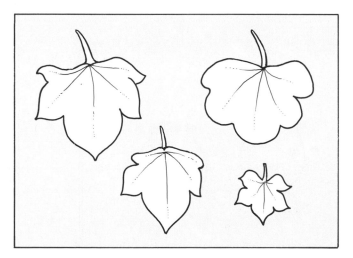

Ivy-leaved toadflax leaves: *roll out some green paste, leaving a slightly thicker part through the middle. If you have a real leaf press it into the paste, then cut round impressions with scissors. Alternatively, choose one of designs above.*

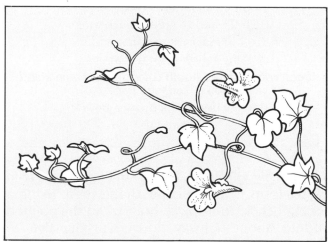

Making a trailing design: *when taping the plant together the usual arrangement is one leaf and one flower coming from the main stem at the same point, but you can vary this slightly to suit your own individual design for your cake.*

Japonica

There are many different varieties of this flower, ranging in colour from a pale shade through to the more familiar vivid coral. The shrub comes into flower before most of the leaves appear, so you only need to make a few leaves for your arrangement.

YOU WILL NEED

Green and white flower paste
20, 24, and 28 green gauge wire
Petal cutter as shown
Tiny yellow-tipped stamens
Green concentrated liquid colouring and gum arabic solution mixed (see page 110)
Coral or deep pink dusting powder
Brown tape

1 First make the calyx. Take a small piece of green paste, form it into a cone shape then, using a cocktail stick (toothpick), hollow out the pointed end to about halfway down. Cut out five 'V' shapes around the rim of the hollowed-out cone, cut off the points and thin down the shapes by rolling them with a cocktail stick (toothpick) against your index finger, taking care not to lose the cone shape of the calyx.

2 Cut a 10 cm (4 in) length of 24 gauge wire, dip it in egg white and pull it through the calyx, pinching the base of the calyx to secure it in position. Place the wire in a piece of polystyrene, sticking it in at an angle to prevent the calyx sliding down the wire before the flower is finished. Work on the petals before the calyx has a chance to dry too much.

3 Roll out some white paste thinly and cut out five petals using the petal cutter. Working on one petal at a time and keeping the others covered, put the petal on the palm of your hand and soften the edge with a balling tool. Transfer the petal to a board and thin down the edges even more by rolling with a cocktail stick (toothpick); recut the petal if it has spread in size. Press with a balling tool to cup slightly, then paint the back of the petal at the base with egg white and place in the calyx. Repeat to make all five petals and position each of them in the calyx.

4 Cut about 15 stamens, just over 1 cm (½ in) in length, and push into the soft paste in the middle of the calyx. Put the wire into a piece of polystyrene at an angle while the flower dries.

5 Make lots of flowers, some with the petals still closed and some with the flowers fully open. Make one or two calyces with just stamens and no petals. Tape the flowers onto a length of 20

Making the calyx: form some green paste into a cone, hollow out the pointed end to about halfway down. Cut out five 'V' shapes around the rim, cut off the points and thin down shapes. Pull wire through calyx, pinching calyx base to secure.

Dragon template for Japonica cake (see page 88)

gauge wire in clusters of two or three. Make a twig with buds (see Twigs, page 100).

6 To make the leaves, cut 5-7.5 cm (2-3 in) lengths of 28 gauge wire. Take some green paste and form a sausage shape for each length of wire. Dip each wire in egg white, then pull it through a sausage shape until the wire is embedded. Roll out the paste on either side of the wire until it is really thin, then cut to the required shape, using a serrated knife to give a rough edge to the leaf. On some of the leaves, curl the edges inwards.

7 Paint the upper side of the leaves with the green colouring and gum arabic solution. Dust the petals and upper part of the calyx with coral or deep pink dusting powder.

8 To make a thorn, cut about 4 cm (1½ in) of brown tape. Roll half the length of the piece into

a sausage shape and taper the end by cutting with scissors. Tape into position beside a cluster of flowers, winding the unrolled part of the tape around the wire.

■ Japonica originally came from China and Japan so for a fun idea when decorating a cake with an arrangement of japonica flowers, make a Chinese dragon using the template above to decorate the side of the cake (see the Japonica cake on page 88). Trace the template onto tracing paper, then prick the outline of the template onto the sugar paste on the sides of the cake. Either colour it in, following the pattern shown on page 88 or devise your own individual dragon pattern.

Single petal cutter

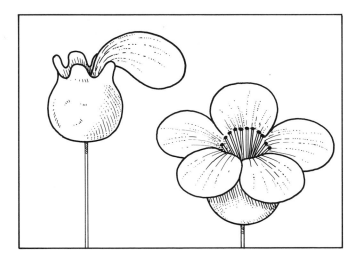

Positioning flowers and stamens: paint the back of the petal at the base with egg white and place in the calyx. Repeat to make all five petals. Cut about 15 stamens, just over 1 cm (½ in) long and push into the paste in middle of the calyx.

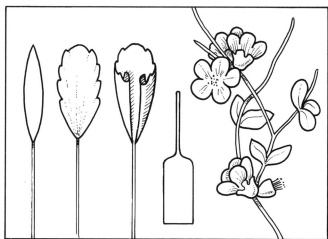

Making leaves and thorns: roll out paste on either side of wire. Cut leaf shape, using a serrated knife to give a rough edge. Curl some edges inwards. For thorns, cut 4 cm (1½ in) of tape, roll half length into a sausage, then taper end.

Larch Fir Cones

These cones are fairly easy to make and look very effective — they make an interesting addition to any autumnal arrangement of leaves and flowers.

YOU WILL NEED

26 gauge brown wire
Light brown flower paste
Dark brown dusting powder
Brown or olive tape

1 Cut several 7.5 cm (3 in) lengths of 26 gauge brown wire and make a hook at one end of each. Dip in egg white and cover the hook with a very small amount of brown paste. Allow the paste to dry overnight.

2 The next day, roll out paste fairly thinly and cut out five small and two large shapes. Work on one at a time, keeping others well covered. Starting with one of the small daisy shapes, roll each petal with a blunt cocktail stick (toothpick) until very thin. Place on some foam and cup just the end with a balling tool.

3 Paint centre of shape with egg white and pull one of wires through so piece of paste is in centre of daisy shape. Close some petals over to cover the paste centre.

4 Continue working the other shapes in the same way, using two more small shapes, then two large, then two more small ones. Try to leave a small space in between by pinching them when in position. When placing the last four shapes put a very small piece of paste between each layer to act as a 'spacer'. Leave to dry, then dust with a darker brown dusting powder. Repeat to make as many cones as you want.

5 To prepare the twig before attaching the cones, cut two lengths of brown wire and tape together with brown or olive tape. Cut several 2.5 cm (1 in) lengths of tape, roll up half the length, then bend the rolled bit over to make a hard bud. Bind the buds onto the wire, starting with one at the end.

6 To make needles, cut 5 cm (2 in) lengths of tape and divide half length of each into three. Twist each piece. Make several, then gather together and tape onto twig.

Medium and small daisy cutter

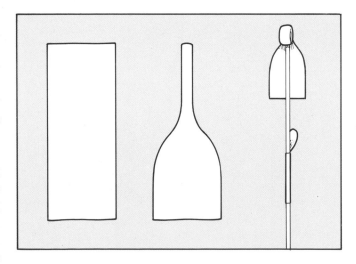

Making the twig: tape together two lengths of brown wire. Cut 2.5 cm (1 in) lengths of tape, roll up half the length, bend over and press to make a hard bud. Bind onto wire, starting with one at the end and grouping the others along the twig.

Lily of the Valley

If time is short, make lots of buds which are quick to make and look very dainty. The 30 gauge wire should be light green. If this is difficult to buy, paint white wire with diluted green paint.

YOU WILL NEED

---

30 and 24 gauge green wire
White flower paste
Green tape

---

1 To make buds, cut 10 cm (4 in) lengths of 30 gauge wire, dip in egg white, and put a tiny piece of paste on the first few, then gradually make the pieces of paste slightly bigger.

2 Once the larger ones are on the wires, mark them with the blunt side of a modelling knife to give the impression of petals which are about to open. Stick the wires in a piece of polystyrene while the buds dry.

3 Cut 7.5 cm (3 in) lengths of 30 gauge wire and make a hook at one end of each. Take a small piece of paste, roll into a ball, then to a pear drop shape. With the pointed end of a cocktail stick

(toothpick), push in the pointed end and roll it against your index finger. Roll again with the blunt end of a cocktail stick (toothpick), keeping a good thickness of paste at the base of the cone to hold the hooked wire securely.

4 Holding the paste at the base, gently cut out six very shallow 'V' shapes and push these points outwards. Inverting this shape, take it between your thumb and index finger then, with a small balling tool, press and turn outwards on each tiny petal in turn.

5 Dip one of the hooked wires in egg white and push it carefully through the flower until the hook is embedded in the thicker paste in the base of the bell-shaped flower.

6 When the wire is in place, put your thumb and index finger at the top of the wire (the back of the flower), and with the index finger on your right hand press gently on the paste in order to regain the flower's bell shape. Repeat the process to make as many flowers as you require for your arrangement. Allow to dry.

7 When all the flowers have dried, tape them together and curve the little stems from the flower head to the main stem. Sometimes it is necessary to add some 24 gauge wire to the 30 gauge wire to give strength to the spray.

Regaining the bell shape: *when wire is in place through the flower, put thumb and index finger at back of flower and with finger on right hand press gently to regain bell shape. When taping together, curve the little stems.*

Lobelia

This beautiful tiny flower makes a lovely change from, or addition to, pulled blossom in a spray. Buds are essential for overall daintiness.

YOU WILL NEED

White, blue, purple and green flower paste (depending on the variety you wish to make)
Cutter as shown
28 gauge green wire
Green tape
White colouring (for blue or purple flowers)

1 With a small piece of white, blue or purple paste, form a Mexican hat (see page 10), making sure that the centre column is both short and very slender. Roll out the paste until very thin and cut out the shape.

2 Put the flower back on the board still upside down, then cut the top petal in two and roll with blunt end of a cocktail stick (toothpick). Turn over and, holding flower by the back part, open up the throat with the sharp end of the cocktail stick (toothpick). Then with blunt end placed over centre, press each petal. Roll each one against index finger of left hand, and indent in centre.

3 Cut a 10 cm (4 in) length of 28 gauge wire and make a small hook at one end. Dip the wire in egg white, then push it through the throat of the flower until the hook is no longer visable. Pinch the back of the flower to keep the hooked wire in place in the paste.

4 To make the calyx, take a very small piece of green paste (pale green for white flowers – much darker for blues and purples) and roll to a long thin cone. With the pointed end of a cocktail stick (toothpick) push well into the cone to open out, then, holding paste against your index finger, roll hard until the edge of the paste is very thin. Cut out five deep 'V' shapes. Pinch and pull out each of these, providing the paste is still pliable. Paint egg white inside the cone, then draw the wire through the cone and position the calyx behind the flower. Tip the flower head slightly.

5 Make buds from long thin cones, but try and leave the rounded part on top. Make indentations with the back of a modelling knife. Put on a calyx, but keep the sepals close to the throat of the bud. Leave to dry, then tape the buds and flowers together.

Lobelia cutter

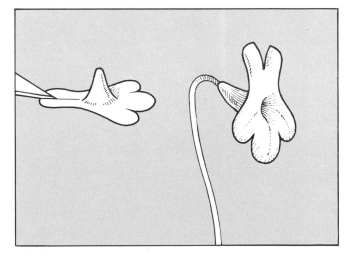

Shaping the petals: *cut top petal into two and roll with blunt cocktail stick (toothpick). Open up throat. Roll bottom petals against index finger of left hand: crease each in centre. Push wire through throat of flower and pinch back of flower.*

Narcissus and Jonquil

YOU WILL NEED

26 gauge pale green wire
Orange, pale yellow, straw-coloured and white flower paste
3 yellow stamens cut to 5 mm (¼ in) long
Yellow dusting powder
Cutter as shown

1 Cut a 7.5 cm (3 in) length of 26 gauge pale green wire and make a hook at one end.

2 To make a narcissus, take a small ball of orange paste and form it into a cone shape, then hollow out with a cocktail stick (toothpick), leaving some thicker paste at the base in which to bury the hook. Placing the little cup on its side on a board, press and frill all round the edge with the blunt end of a cocktail stick (toothpick). Dip stamens in egg white and then in yellow dusting powder. Dip the wire hook in the egg white, push into the little cup and pinch the base of the cone to keep it in place. Using tweezers, position the little stamens. Place in a polystyrene block.

3 Roll out some pale yellow paste and cut out two petal shapes. Keep one covered while you work on the other. Quickly press the edges with a balling tool on your hand, then place on board and roll from the centre to edge of each petal with a cocktail stick (toothpick).

4 Put a little egg white on the back of the orange cup and thread the petals into place behind it. Repeat with the second shape, paint a small amount of egg white in the centre and slide the petals up the wire and position so that petals show between the first petals. Twist some of the petals to give the feeling of movement. Bend the wire behind the flower head.

5 Take a small piece of straw-coloured paste and roll out thinly, then cut out a very small oval shape. Mark the shape all over with anything that will make fine lines. Crumple a little, then paint egg white on the base and stick onto the wire just behind the flower head. Make a jonquil as above only using white paste. Make several heads, tape together, and at the base of the stems fix on the straw-coloured bud cover.

Snowdrop cutter

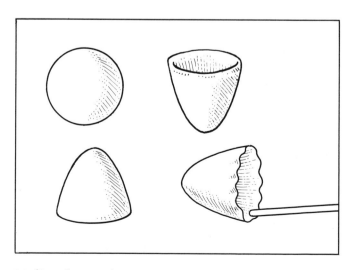

Making the cup shape: *form a small ball of orange paste into a cone shape, then hollow out the broad end with a cocktail stick (toothpick). Place the cup on its side on a board and frill all round the edge with blunt end of a cocktail stick.*

51

Nasturtium

Nasturtiums come in a wonderful array of colours. If the flowers are likely to be anywhere damp, do not make them in the darker shades as they are more likely to lose their shape and flop than the paler colours.

YOU WILL NEED

30 gauge white wire and 24 and 28 gauge green wire
Flower paste which can be anything from cream through to yellow and deep orange, plus green paste
8 fine yellow stamens for each flower
Crumpled white crêpe paper
Green concentrated liquid colouring mixed with gum arabic solution (see page 110)
White concentrated liquid colouring mixed with pale green

1 Cut a 10 cm (4 in) length of 30 gauge white wire. Take some of the coloured paste of your choice of colour for the flowers and form it into a sausage shape. Dip the wire in egg white and pull it through the sausage of paste.

2 Roll out the paste on either side of the wire until it is extremely thin, leaving a thicker part, about 5 mm (¼ in) thick, at the wire end. The wire must only be about 2.5 cm (1 in) into the paste; if it still shows in the middle of the petal, put your thumb one side and your index finger at the back, press gently together and firmly ease the wire away.

3 Place the petal over your finger and roll just the edge with a cocktail stick (toothpick) to give the petal a feeling of movement and make the paste very thin.

4 Place the petal between two pieces of white crêpe paper and press gently to curve the whole petal. Allow to dry. Make one more petal in the same way.

5 Make a third petal the same way but slit open the thicker part of the petal, and thin down this flap of paste, taking care as you open up this petal (see Making a fringed petal).

6 With scissors, cut a fringe and if possible flick up the paste between the slits. Thin the petal by rolling the edge with a cocktail stick (toothpick), the place between two pieces of white crêpe paper and press gently to curve this petal in the same way as with the first two. Make two more petals in the same way – you should then have two plain and three fringed petals.

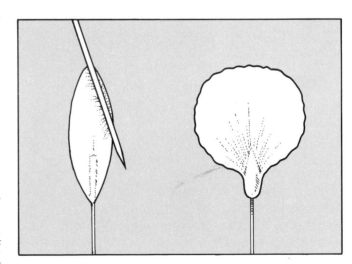

Rolling out the paste: roll out the paste on either side of the wire until it is extremely thin, leaving a thicker part about 5 mm (¼ in) thick at the wire end. The wire must only be about 2.5 cm (1 in) into the paste and not show through.

7 When all the petals are dry, cut two 10 cm (4 in) lengths of 24 gauge green wire. Group the petals with the two plain ones together and the three fringed ones opposite (see Positioning the petals) and tape the 30 gauge white wire that the petals are on to the green wires.

8 To make the calyx, take a piece of cream paste and form it into a long cone. Hollow out the blunt end with a cocktail stick (toothpick), then cut five 'V' shapes in this end. Thin down each of the 'V' shapes with a blunt cocktail stick (toothpick). Pull the petals on their wires through the calyx at an angle (see Making the calyx), then put a curve into the spur of the calyx towards the stem. Push eight stamens into the centre of the flower before the calyx dries.

9 To make the leaves, cut three or five 10 cm (4 in) lengths of 28 gauge green wire and tape them together, starting about 1 cm (½ in) from the top. Splay out the top 1 cm (½ in) of the wires and gently curve the very end of each one upwards at a 90° angle so that they will be able to hold the large circular leaf. Roll out some green paste fairly thinly, cut out a rough circle and thin the edge until extremely fine.

10 Paint the splayed wires with egg white and place the circle of paste on top, making sure that the wires do not come to the edge of the paste.

Press the leaves into place gently and allow to dry before painting.

11 When all the leaves are completely dry, paint with green concentrated liquid colouring mixed with gum arabic solution and mark veins radiating out from the centre by taking off the wet paint with the blunt end of a cocktail stick (toothpick). Alternatively, wait until the leaves are dry, and paint the veins in with white colouring mixed with pale green colouring.

Positioning the petals: when all the petals are dry, cut two 10 cm (4 in) lengths of 24 gauge green wire. Group the petals with the two plain ones together and the three fringed ones opposite and tape them to the wires.

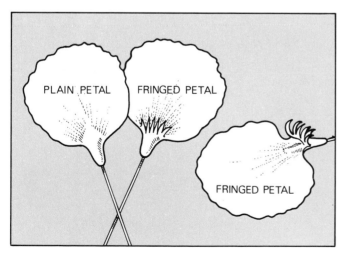

Making a fringed petal: make the petal in the same way as the plain petal, but slit open the thicker part of the petal and thin down this flap of paste, taking care as you open up this petal. Cut a fringe and if possible flick up the fringes.

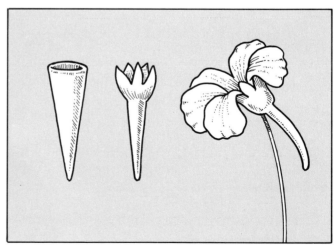

Making the calyx: form cream paste into a long cone and hollow out blunt end with a cocktail stick (toothpick). Cut five 'V' shapes in this end and thin down. Pull the petals through calyx at an angle, then curve spur of calyx towards the stem.

area (see Making the petals), with a cocktail stick (toothpick).

4 Brush the bottom of the petal (the dotted area shown on the diagram, see Making the petals) with egg white and place one of the wires with the piece of paste on it in the centre. Bring round both sides of the petal so that the two edges meet at the base. Carefully bend the top of the petal back slightly. Stick the wire into a piece of polystyrene while making rest of petals.

Making the petals: cut out a single petal (shape 'A'). Frill the edge (the shaded area in the diagram) with a cocktail stick (toothpick). Brush bottom of petal, the dotted area, with egg white and place the wire with piece of paste on it in the centre.

Orchid

These instructions given here are for the dainty, small orchid which comes in a variety of colours, ranging from a very pale cream to a richer mauve colour.

YOU WILL NEED

28 gauge green wire
Flower paste of your choice of colour (see introduction)
Cutters as shown
Dusting powders of various colours
Green tape

1 Cut several 7.5 cm (3 in) lengths of 28 gauge green wire and make a hook at one end of each using tweezers.

2 Take a very small piece of paste and cover the hook on the wires. Curve slightly at the end and allow to dry.

3 Roll out some more paste of your choice of colour for the petals until it is very thin and cut out a single petal (shape 'A'). Frill the edge, the shaded

Shaping the petal: bring round both sides of petal so the two edges meet at the base. Bend top of petal back. Cut out shape 'B'. Thin edges, then place on foam and cup the petals, shaping three back and two forward.

5 Roll out some more paste and cut out shape 'B'. Thin the petal edges either with a cocktail stick (toothpick) or a balling tool, then place on a piece of foam and press each of the petals in turn with a balling tool to cup the petals, shaping three back and two forward.

6 Paint the back of shape 'A' with egg white, then slide shape 'B' up the wire and position it behind shape 'A'.

7 Leave the flower to dry completely. Repeat to make as many flowers as you want, add markings, then tape them onto another length of wire.

■ This orchid is not meant to portray any specific species. The arrangement of most orchids is three petals and three sepals i.e. three sepals and two petals behind and the lip coming forward which is the third petal. You can create many different types of flowers just by cutting and frilling the lip and petals, or leaving them plain, by bringing some forward and positioning some back.

Cutter 'A' (left); cutter 'B' (right)

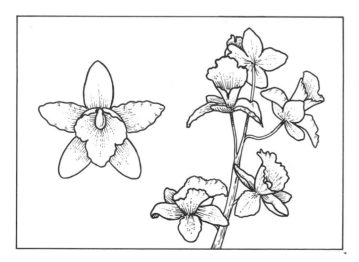

Finishing the flowers: leave the flower to dry completely. Repeat to make as many flowers as you want, add the markings with liquid colouring or dusting powder, then tape them onto another length of wire.

Pansy

It is a good idea to make several flowers at the same time, so that some petals have a chance to dry while you are working on others.

YOU WILL NEED

26 gauge green wire
Pale green tape
Flower paste of your choice of colour, plus mid-green paste
Cutters as shown
Small yellow stamens
Green concentrated liquid colouring mixed with gum arabic solution (see page 110)
Dusting powder slightly darker than your choice of colours

1 Cut two 10 cm (4 in) lengths of 26 gauge wire and a third piece about 5 mm (¼ in) longer than the other two. Tape them together.

2 Roll out the paste of your choice, not too thinly, then cut out the individual petal shape, using the cutter. Thin the edge with a balling tool, then place the broad edge of the petal over your index finger and really thin down the paste by rolling it with a cocktail stick (toothpick) to make the petal a rounder shape.

3 Paint the narrow end of the petal with egg white and wrap this part of the petal around the wire (see Shaping first petal). Allow to dry.

4 Repeat to make two more petals, and fix them behind the first petal. Position these petals so that they nearly touch each other (see Positioning the last petals).

5 Cut out two more petal shapes. Again thin the edges, then place them behind the first three petals. Generally, looking at the flower, put on the right-hand petal first, and lastly, the left-hand petal. The petals sometimes overlap the other way i.e. left in front of right. The second part of a sweet pea (see page 70) can be used as petals 2 and 3 and 4 and 5, if preferred. It may be necessary to bend the wire down in order to position the last two petals. The points of the petals of the pansy flower will not always lie in line with each other.

6 Position a small yellow stamen so that it just shows in the throat of the flower. Allow all the petals to dry.

7 Bend the wire down, if not already done. Make a small cone of the same colour paste as the flower, and stick the cone on directly behind the petals below the bend in the wire. Allow these cones to dry.

8 Meanwhile, make the calyx. The calyx is a fairly complicated structure to copy in superpaste, but by only making the last two sepals (sepals are the separate parts that make up the calyx) as near to nature as possible, it should give the impression of the correct formation. Roll out some green paste and cut out several calyx shapes for each flower, using the cutter. Taking one calyx, cut away two sections (see Finishing the flower), then thin down edges of remaining three. Paint with egg white, then fix behind the upper petals.

9 Take two more calyces and cut off one sepal shape from each, taking the centre part of the calyx as well (see Finishing the flower). Thin down with a cocktail stick (toothpick), paint with egg white and fix one either side of the wire, pointing the opposite way to the three sepals.

10 To make the leaves, cut one 5 cm (2 in) length of 28 gauge wire for each leaf you want to make. Take some mid-green paste and form it into a sausage shape. Dip one of the wires into egg white and pull through the paste until only about 1 cm (½ in) is still embedded in the paste. Roll out the paste very gently over the wire and more firmly either side, until the paste is very thin but the wire is not showing.

11 Cut to shape with scissors; most of the leaves have a slightly 'toothed' edge and this is best

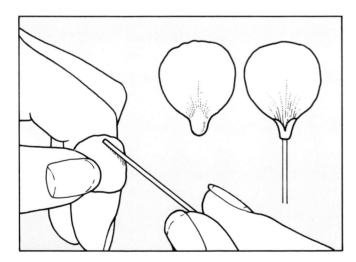

Shaping first petal: roll out paste, not too thinly, then cut out petal shape. Thin edge with a balling tool, then place broad edge over index finger and thin with cocktail stick (toothpick). Paint narrow end with egg white and wrap round the wire.

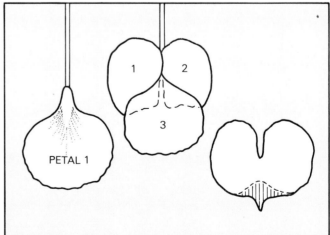

Cutting remaining petals: cut out two more petal shapes, then fix behind first petal, so they nearly touch each other. Cut out two more, thin edges and place behind others. Cutter for second part of sweet pea can be used for these, if preferred.

achieved with scissors. Mark on the veins with a modelling tool. Allow to dry. When dry, paint the spaces in between the veins, allowing the lighter colour of the veins to show through and give a life-like effect.

12 To make buds, cut lengths of wire as for the open flowers, make a hook at one end of each and dip in egg white. Take some paste of the same colour as you are using for the flowers and form it into small sausage shapes, then pull a wire through each one. Allow to dry.

13 Roll out some paste and cut out two petal shapes. Thin down the edge of one of the petals and wrap it around the sausage shape. Thin down the second petal, paint it with egg white, and place loosely over the first petal and the sausage shape, gently pinching it at the edge a couple of times to secure it.

14 Bend the wire as before and make a calyx in the same way as for open flowers, but this time cutting two sepals together, and then fixing three shapes in the spaces in between.

15 When all the petals and buds are dry, shade the petals with darker coloured dusting powder. In the case of the buds, take the colour down over the calyx as well. When flowers are coloured, tape the flowers, buds and leaves together.

Left to right: part of sweet pea cutter, individual petal cutter, calyx cutter

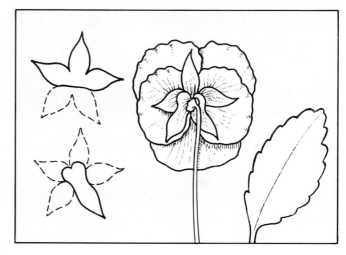

Finishing the flower: cut out calyx shapes, cut away two sections, thin down edges of remaining three and fix behind upper petals. Cut out two shapes from two calyces and fix either side of wire. Cut out leaves to get a 'toothed' edge.

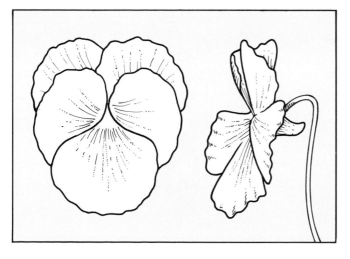

Positioning the last petals: If necessary bend the wire down to position the last two petals. Position a small yellow stamen so that it just shows in the throat of the flower. Make a small cone of same colour paste and stick on behind petals.

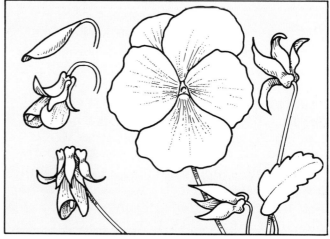

Making buds: form paste into sausage shapes, then pull a wire through each. Roll out some paste and cut out two petals. Thin edge of one and wrap it around sausage shape. Thin second petal, paint with egg white and place over first petal.

Plantain

Making the stamens is the most difficult part of making a plantain, but only a few heads are needed in an arrangement as on the Buttercup cake (see page 80).

YOU WILL NEED

24 gauge green wire
Green tape
White stamen cotton
Cream and brownish/green flower paste
Egg white or vegetable fat (shortening)

1 Cut two 10 cm (4 in) lengths of 24 gauge wire, tape together and make a hook at one end. Cut 1 cm (½ in) lengths of stamen cotton.

2 Roll some cream paste into a long, very thin sausage shape and cut diagonally into short lengths, about 2.5 mm (⅛ in). Work on one length at a time and keep the rest covered. Dip one end of a stamen in egg white and push into a piece of paste. Repeat to make lots of these.

3 Take some brownish/green paste and soften it by adding a little egg white and white vegetable

fat. Form it into a sausage shape. Dip the hooked wire in egg white and pull it through the sausage shape of paste. Push the stamens into this paste to make a ring all the way round it at any level (see Making the stamen ring). The stamens start showing at the base, then gradually work up the head, dying off as new ones come out higher up – so the ring of stamens moves up.

4 Roughen up the remainder of the plantain head by pinching at the paste with tweezers.

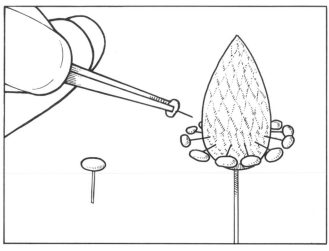

Making the stamen ring: soften some brownish/green paste with egg white and white vegetable fat, then form into a pointed sausage shape. Dip hooked wire in egg white and pull through paste. Push stamens into this paste to make a ring.

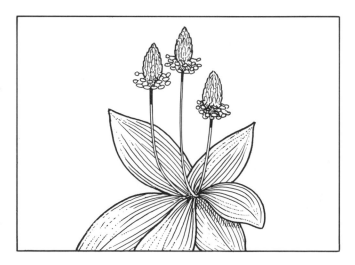

Finishing the head: stamens start showing at base, then work up the head, dying off as new ones come out higher up – the ring of stamens moves up as spring and summer progress. Roughen up remainder of head by pinching with tweezers.

Poinsettia

It is difficult to get the flowers true to life as they are irregular in shape and tinged with yellow. Concentrate instead on the bracts (modified leaves) which are red and green but can also be white and pink.

YOU WILL NEED

28 and 30 gauge green wire
Red thread
Yellow dusting powder
Green and red flower paste
Green tape

1 Cut a 7.5 cm (3 in) length of 30 gauge wire and place it alongside a cocktail stick (toothpick), then wind red thread around both of them about four or five times. Pull the wire down either side of the loop of thread and twist it (see Making the stamens). Slide the thread off the cocktail stick (toothpick) and tie the thread just above where the wire goes through, then cut the threads.

2 Brush the top of the stamens with egg white and dip in yellow dusting powder.

3 Take some green paste and form into a small cone. Slightly hollow out the flat end of the paste cone with a cocktail stick (toothpick), then pull the stamens and wires down through the cone and press into place. Repeat to make several flowers and tape at least three together.

4 Cut twelve to fourteen 7.5 cm (3 in) lengths of 28 gauge green wire. Form a small thin sausage shape of red paste. Dip one of the wires in egg white and pull it through the paste until the wire is well in. Roll out the paste on either side of the wire with a cocktail stick (toothpick) until the edge is very thin.

5 Take care not to roll over the wire too much or it will break the surface. Trim with fine scissors to make the leaf shape and make sure it has a fine point. Mark a vein down through the leaf as deep as possible, then mark the side veins with a little less pressure.

6 Continue making leaves in this way, getting progressively larger. Use a balling tool to stretch out the edges to form irregular shapes and trim the shape with scissors where necessary (see Making the leaves).

7 With the bigger bracts, make the edges slightly irregular. Make odd numbers of each size, as even numbers will give a square shape, for example

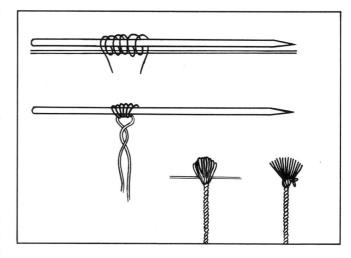

Making the stamens: wind thread around cocktail stick (toothpick) and wire four or five times. Pull wire down either side of loop of thread and twist it. Slide thread off cocktail stick (toothpick), tie above where wire goes through; cut threads.

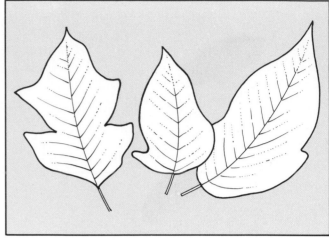

Making the flowers: *take some green paste and form into a small cone. Slightly hollow out the cone, then pull the stamens and wires down through the cone and press into place. Repeat to make several flowers and tape at least three together.*

Making larger leaves: *with the bigger leaves, make the edges slightly irregular. Keep the numbers of each size odd, as even numbers will give a square shape i.e. three small, five medium and three large. Finish with three irregular leaves.*

make three small, five medium and three large. Finish with three green leaves of an irregular shape (see Making larger leaves).

8 If you want the poinsettia to lie close to the cake in your arrangement, tape the flowers and bracts closer together than on the real plant.

■ During the past few years this lovely plant with its distinctive brilliant red leaves has become an increasingly popular part of the Christmas scene. Whereas at one time it was only to be seen on

Christmas cards, now it frequently has pride of place in many homes during the festive season and carries on to bring a little colour into what can be a drab time of year.

For cake decorating purposes it is best kept scaled down from the real size. The tiny flowers are quite complicated, but it is sufficient just to give the impression of the small green cups, red stamens and yellow pollen surrounded by lots of bright red, cream or pink bracts. It is best not to use cutters but just to cut the shapes with scissors as they vary so much.

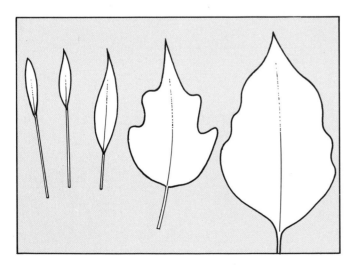

Making the leaves: *pull wire through sausage of red paste. Roll out paste either side of wire until edge is very thin. Trim with scissors to make the leaf shape, then mark veins. Continue making leaves, getting progressively larger.*

Taping the leaves (bracts) together: *if you want the poinsettia to lie close to the cake in your decorative arrangement, tape the flowers and colourful leaves (bracts) closer together than they are on the real plant.*

Poppy

This well-loved, dramatic flower is best made with white paste and painted red when dry, as red-coloured paste can attract damp.

YOU WILL NEED

24 gauge green wire
Green tape
Green and white flower paste
Fine black stamens
Cutter as shown
Red and black, brown or dark green colouring
Brown dusting powder (optional)

1 Cut two 10 cm (4 in) lengths of 24 gauge wire, tape them together and make a hook at one end.

2 Take a small piece of green paste and shape it into a cone. Dip the taped wire into egg white, then pull it through the cone, starting from the flat end, until the hook is embedded in the paste and the straight part of the wire hangs down from the pointed end of the cone.

3 Using tweezers, pinch the paste on the top (flat part) of the cone to make ridges radiating out from the centre, then pinch around the edge so that it looks like a lid.

4 Cut the black stamens in varying lengths, bend slightly to curve them, then push them about 5 mm (¼ in) into the cone to make the poppy centre. Allow to dry overnight.

5 Roll out a piece of white paste fairly thiny. Cut out the poppy shape with a cutter. Place the paste on your hand and, working quickly, soften the edges with a balling tool. Place on a board then, using a cocktail stick (toothpick), work from the centre of the petals outwards to really thin down the edges. Extra pressure on the cocktail stick (toothpick) will achieve a slight frilling effect. Place the shape on a piece of foam. Using a balling tool, apply slight pressure to each petal to form it into a curved shape.

6 Paint both sides of the two large petals with egg white. Bring the two smaller petals forward and stick the larger petals behind. This will automatically make the whole flower into a bowl shape.

7 Paint the poppy centre with egg white just below the level of the stamens. Pull the wire through the petals so the stamens are in the centre, then press the petals into place around the base of the cone. Immediately hang the flower upside-down to dry.

Making the poppy centre: *pinch the paste on the top of the cone of paste to make ridges radiating out from the centre, then pinch around the edge so that it looks like a lid. Cut the stamens, bend slightly and push 5 mm (¼ in) into the cone.*

8 When dry, the flower can be painted with red colouring, adding black, brown or dark green colouring to the base of the petals. It is sometimes difficult to paint between the stamens, so use a small brush. Paint the raised parts of the centre cone with brown colouring or dust with brown dusting powder.

Poppy cutter

Making the flower shapes: paint both sides of the two large petals with egg white. Bring the two smaller petals forward and stick the larger petals behind, securing them with the egg white. This will make the flower into a bowl shape.

Primrose

These delicate flowers need to be very finely moulded. The depth of colour varies from very pale to deeper yellow. Instructions for leaves are given on page 100.

YOU WILL NEED

26 gauge pale green wire
Yellow and pale green flower paste
Wooden honiton bobbin
Primrose cutter and one of the snowdrop cutters as shown
Dark yellow colouring

1 Cut a piece of 26 gauge wire about 7.5 cm (3 in) long and make a hook at one end. Take a small piece of yellow paste, roll into a ball, then form into a Mexican hat shape on the board (see page 10). Using a cocktail stick (toothpick), roll out the paste round the edge very thinly, leaving the centre column.

2 Lift the shape off the board with a palette knife and very gently thin down the centre column of paste by rolling it between your thumb and index finger.

3 Put it back on the board and place the primrose cutter on it, making sure that the column is in the centre. Cut out the shape and lift off the board. Turn the Mexican hat upside down and open up the centre column, now the throat of the flower, using first the pointed end of a cocktail stick (toothpick), then the blunt end.

4 Holding the primrose head in your left hand, and supporting the petals on your index finger, roll hard on each half of the heart-shaped petals in turn, working from the centre to the side, thus retaining the shape. At this point, decide whether you want the primrose petals to lie right back as a completely open flower, or curl inwards slightly for a half-open flower (see Making open and half-open flowers).

5 Dip the wire hook in egg white, then thread the wire through the flower, making sure the hook is well down the throat. Push the pale green stamen into the flower so it is flush with the primrose petals. Allow to dry.

6 When the flower is dry, paint the centre of the flower a darker yellow.

7 To make buds, make as above, but then push the petals upright. For tighter buds, cut out with the part of a snowdrop cutter illustrated and roll the petals hard so that they curl back on themselves. Push the wire down through the petals, then gently push petals into a tighter formation round the wire.

8 To make the calyx, take a very small amount of green paste, roll it into a ball, then make a point at one end. With the sharp end of a cocktail stick (toothpick), open up the pointed end of the paste, rolling against the index finger of your left hand, then reverse the cocktail stick (toothpick) and roll with the blunt end inside. Cut out five 'V' shapes and re-roll the paste. Paint the inside of the calyx with a little egg white and then slide it up the wire until it is positioned partly over the throat of the flower.

9 With tweezers, pinch the full length of the calyx either side of the points. Pinch the calyx carefully at the bottom to make it stay in place below the flower on the wire.

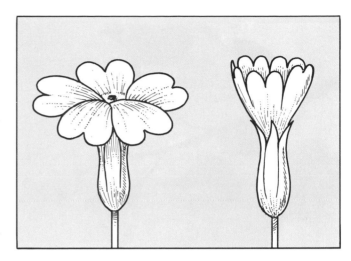

Making open and half-open flowers: *supporting the petals on your index finger, roll hard on each half of the petals in turn, working from centre to side, then make petals lie back as an open flower or curl inwards for a half-open flower.*

Primrose cutter (left); snowdrop cutter (right)

Finishing the flower: *with tweezers, pinch the full length of the calyx either side of the points. Pinch the calyx carefully at the bottom to make is stay in place on the wire. Make leaves, if wished, following the instructions on page 100.*

Rose

If you want texturing on your rose, press each petal between two pieces of white crepe paper, remembering to keep the lines going the same way.

YOU WILL NEED

24 gauge green wire
Flower paste of your choice of colour, plus lighter and darker green paste
Cutters as shown
Polystyrene tray (the sort apples are sold in), if making a fuller rose

1 Cut a 10 cm (4 in) length of 24 gauge wire and make a hook at one end. Dip the wire in egg white and pull it through a small piece of paste that is slightly pointed at one end. Allow this flower centre to dry overnight.

2 Roll out some of the paste of your choice and cut out about 15 petals (you may not need them all), using individual petal cutter. Work on one petal at a time, keeping others well covered.

3 Dip the flower centre in egg white and stick the wire into a piece of polystyrene. Thin down the edge of the first petal by rolling it with a cocktail stick (toothpick), then place the petal behind the flower centre, sticking it well on the left hand side. Roll the cocktail stick (toothpick) over the petal to make it stick completely (you should not be able to see the blob in the centre). Don't worry about covering base of centre with the first.

4 Take the second petal and thin the top and right hand edge with a balling tool. Paint with egg white (see Positioning first two petals) and place over the edge of the first petal, sticking only one side down.

5 Prepare the next petal in the same way and tuck this inside the free, unstuck edge of the second petal. Paint a little egg white inside points 'A' and 'B'; press down with cocktail stick (toothpick).

6 Put on the next two petals in the same way, only placing new petals where the last two finished.

7 To make a more realistic curve on the edge of each petal from the third one on, thin down the top edge, turn the petal over and run a small balling tool from the point to near the curved edge. Only paint egg white on lower part of petal and turn edge of the petal over on two sides.

8 Ideally the calyx should be a lighter green on the inside than on the outside. To achieve this, take two pieces of thin green paste, one dark and

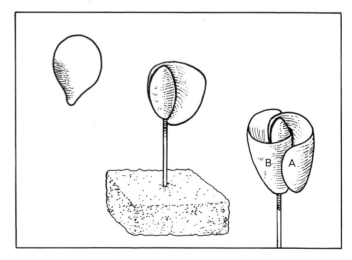

Positioning first two petals: place first petal behind flower centre, rolling it with cocktail stick (toothpick) to make it stick. Paint second petal with egg white (the dotted area shown above) and place over edge of first petal with right side left free.

one light, put one on top of the other and roll hard together and cut out the calyx shape using the cutter. If you are making lots of roses the same colour, make sure you have enough two-toned green paste.

9 Thin the edges of the calyx and either cut out points on sepals, or press pointed end of cocktail stick (toothpick) into the paste and twist. Ball each sepal to make them curve, paint with egg white and fix into position. Fix a piece of paste underneath same colour as outside of calyx.

10 If you want to make a tight rose, do not turn the petals back, but slightly frill the last five to seven petals by thinning top edge in usual way, then rolling a blunt cocktail stick (toothpick) right on the edge but not all the way round.

11 To make a fuller rose, cut out about nine petals and prepare in the same way as above, then allow to dry. Make a rose bud with another six to eight petals. Grease the polystyrene tray, make a hole in the centre and place a green calyx in it. Make up a glue mixture by mixing some of the paste used for the petals with egg white until it is the consistency of thick royal icing. Put a little of this glue in the centre of the calyx and place the dry petals on it, then pull the rose bud on its wire through the middle and through the hole in tray. Secure wire and leave to dry.

Rose petal cutter (left); calyx cutter (right)

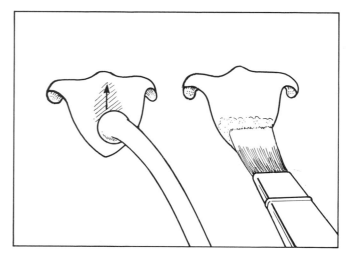

Curving petals: *to make realistic curve on edge of each petal from the third one on, thin down top edge, turn petal over and run balling tool from point to near curved edge. Paint egg white on lower part of petal and turn edge over on two sides.*

Positioning remaining petals: *prepare next petal same way and tuck inside free edge of second petal. Paint egg white inside points 'A' and 'B'; press with cocktail stick (toothpick). Continue placing new petals where last two finished.*

Cutting the calyx and frilling petals: *two sepals have cuts either side, one has cuts on the right, one on the left and one has none at all. To make a tight rose, don't turn petals back but frill last five to seven by rolling on top edge.*

Snowdrop

The outer petals are almost twice the length of the inner petals in real life, but look too overwhelming if you make them that size for a cake, so use a little artistic licence and make them a bit smaller.

YOU WILL NEED

26 gauge green wire
White and green flower paste
Yellow stamen cotton
Cutters as shown
Green colouring

1 Cut a 10 cm (4 in) length of 26 gauge wire and make a hook at one end. Dip the hook in egg white and cover with a tiny piece of white paste. Cut three tiny pieces of yellow stamen cotton, each about 5 mm (¼ in) long, and push them into the centre of the piece of paste using a pair of tweezers.

2 Roll out a small amount of white paste until it is thin and cut out petal shapes 'A' and 'B'. Put shape 'A' in the palm of your hand and thin the edge with a balling tool then, applying a small amount of pressure, take from the outer edge of

the petal to the centre to curve the petal (see Making the petals).

3 Paint egg white on the centre of 'A', then thread the wire through centre until the petals slide onto the piece of paste and the stamens are positioned in the centre of the flower.

4 Thin the edges of shape 'B' in the same way with a balling tool, then place on a piece of foam. Apply pressure with the balling tool, working from each of the points to the centre in the middle of the three petals in order to curve the paste slightly.

5 Paint the centre of shape 'B' with egg white, then thread the wire holding the stamens and the first three petals through this shape and position these longer petals in between the petals of shape 'A'.

6 Take a small piece of green paste and hollow it slightly with a cocktail stick (toothpick). Paint the hollow with egg white, then slide it up the wire to fix the hollow part to the back of the flower. Using a pair of tweezers, carefully bend the wire just above the flower head.

7 Make a long, very fine sausage shape of green paste and then cut to about 1.5 cm (¾ in) long. With the shape on the board, press a cocktail

Making the petals: apply a small amount of pressure with a balling tool from outer edge to centre of shape 'A' to curve petals. Thread wire through centre. Work from point to centre of shape 'B' to curve, then position these between 'A' petals.

stick (toothpick) along the length of the sausage shape, to make the centre thin enough to look translucent. Paint one end of the shape with egg white, then fix it just below the bend of the stem, bringing the snowdrop to the board rather than trying to take the very fragile paste shape to the flower, and curve the green shape to form the bud cover (or spathe).

8 When the flower is dry, paint the inner petals with little lines of green colouring. There are various markings for different varieties – try to copy a real snowdrop if possible.

■ The familiar drooping white flowers of the common snowdrop are among the first flowers of the year, often appearing in its favourite haunts of damp woods and orchards when the snow is still on the ground. The snowdrop is also known by the delightful name of February fair-maid, and its Latin name, *Galanthus nivalis*, means milk-flower of the snow.

Cutter 'A' (left); cutter 'B' (right)

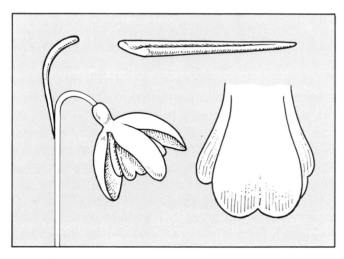

Making the bract and colouring the petals: *press a cocktail stick (toothpick) along length of sausage shape to make centre thin enough to look translucent. Fix onto stem. When flower is dry, paint petals with green colouring.*

Spindle berry

This tree/shrub has very attractive berries and leaves which turn different autumnal shades.

YOU WILL NEED

24 and 28 gauge green wire
Pink/coral and cream flower paste
Slightly darker pink/coral dusting powder
Light brown, red and/or yellow concentrated liquid colouring
Gum arabic solution (see page 110)
Brown tape

1 Cut some 7.5 cm (3 in) lengths of 24 gauge wire and make a hook at one end of each.

2 Form some pink/coral paste into a large pea shape. Dip the wire in egg white and pull through the paste until the hook is embedded. Shape the paste with a modelling tool to divide it into four or five lobes. Allow to dry, then shade by dusting with slightly darker dusting powder.

3 To make the leaves, form some cream paste into a sausage shape about 2.5 cm (1 in) long. Dip one of the wires in egg white and pull it through the paste. Roll out paste either side of wire until really thin, then cut to the required shape.

4 Rub the edge of the leaf with a balling tool to make the shape look natural and not stiff. Paint on different colours – light brown, red and/or yellow. Allow to dry, then paint with gum arabic solution. While the gum arabic solution is still wet, mark main vein with the blunt end of a cocktail stick (toothpick). Tape the leaves and berries together with brown tape.

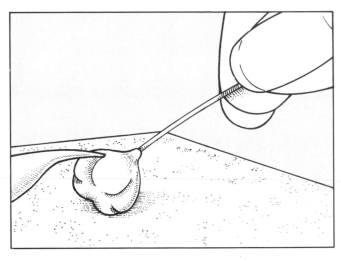

Making the berries: *pull the wire through the pea-shaped piece of paste until hook is embedded. Shape the paste with a modelling tool to divide it into four or five lobes. Allow to dry, then shade by dusting with slightly darker dusting powder.*

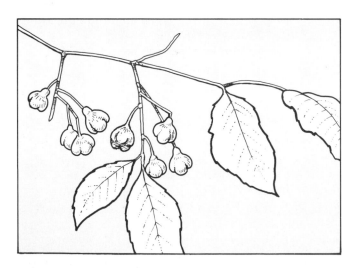

Making leaf edges: *rub the edge of the leaf with a balling tool to make shape look natural and not stiff. Paint on different colours, allow to dry, then paint with gum arabic solution and mark veins. Tape leaves and berries together.*

Summer Jasmine

Make lots of buds as these are very attractive, especially in formal sprays. Outdoor varieties have a calyx, but hothouse ones do not seem to.

YOU WILL NEED

24 gauge green wire
White and green flower paste
Cutter as shown
Brown and pink dusting powder

1 Cut several 7.5 cm (3 in) lengths of 24 gauge wire and make a hook at one end of each. Take a piece of white paste and form it into a Mexican hat shape (see page 10). Place the cutter over it, press hard and twist to cut out the shape. Make sure the central column (which will be the throat of the flower) is thin, then lift the shape off the board with a palette knife.

2 Open up the throat with the pointed end of a cocktail stick (toothpick), and then with the blunt end. Lean the cocktail stick (toothpick) briefly against each petal – rest the blunt end of the stick over the throat, roll half of each petal, and then the other half, over the index finger of your left hand. This method should retain the shape of the petals. Slightly twist at least three of the petals.

3 Dip a hooked wire in egg white and push it through the throat of the flower until the hook is out of sight. Colour with dusting powder when dry, remembering that the brown/pink colouring is on the upper side of each flower.

4 To make buds, take some white paste and form it into small sausage shapes. Dip a hooked wire in egg white and pull it through the paste until the hook is embedded. Thin down the end of the sausage shape nearest the wire and make a point at the other end.

5 To make a calyx, take a very small piece of green paste and form it into a thin cone. Open up the blunt end with a cocktail stick (toothpick) and cut five 'V' shapes around the edge. Roll each of them with a cocktail stick (toothpick) against the index finger of your left hand. Paint the inside with egg white and slide up the wire to position behind a flower or bud, pinching the base slightly to keep the calyx in place on the wire.

Summer jasmine petal cutter

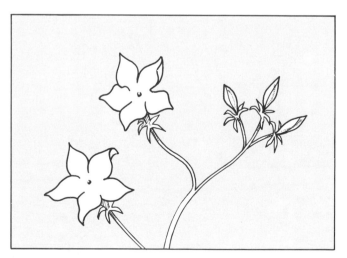

Positioning the calyces: paint the inside of each shaped and rolled calyx with egg white and slide it up the wire to position behind either a flower or bud, pinching the base slightly to keep the calyx in place.

Sweet Pea

Lovely colours and long straight stems, with occasional tendrils are the main features of these pretty summer flowers. Three different cutters are used to make this flower.

YOU WILL NEED

Flower paste of your choice of colour, plus green paste
Dusting powder of your choice of colour
24 and 30 or 33 gauge wire
3 cutters as shown
Small star cutter (optional)

1 Cut several 10 cm (4 in) lengths of 24 gauge wire and make a hook at one end of each. Dip each hook in egg white and cover with a tiny piece of the paste of your choice.

2 To make each flower, roll out the paste of your choice thinly and cut out petal shape 'A'. Soften the edge with a balling tool, mark the centre with a crease, then paint egg white around the edges. Fold the petal around the tiny piece of paste on the end of the wire, with the pointed end of the petal at the base. Make sure the tiny piece of paste on the wire is completely covered by the petal. Pull the top of the petal backwards (see Making the first petal).

3 Cut out shape 'B', ball edges in same way, then roll a cocktail stick (toothpick) around edge, keeping stick in line with bottom point of petal, to thin edge. Cup petals with balling tool, working from outside edge to centre. Mark centre with a crease, paint with egg white at base to 5 mm (¼ in) up petal. Place this petal behind the first one and pinch it to keep it in position.

4 Cut out shape 'C', ball the edge and thin with a cocktail stick (toothpick) as before. Mark a crease through centre, paint on egg white and place behind the second petal. Take the top of the petal where the crease is and pull back firmly.

5 To make the calyx, roll out some green paste and cut out a star shape using a star cutter. Alternatively, form a calyx with five sepals from a ball of green paste using the pulled flower method (see page 10). Pull the wire with the petals on through the calyx to position the calyx behind the petals.

6 Repeat to make three/five flower heads and allow to dry. When dry, shade with dusting powder, then tape them together.

7 To make the tendrils, cut out three 10 cm (4 in) lengths of 30 or 33 gauge wire and tape together, leaving about 5 cm (2 in) for each tendril. Curve the ends round a cocktail stick (toothpick), then join the curved tendrils at the base of the flower stem.

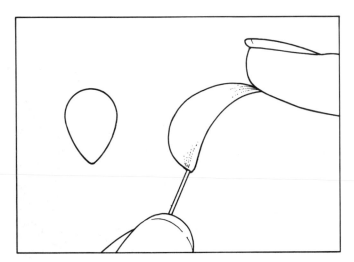

Making the first petal: cut out petal shape 'A' and soften edge. Mark centre with a crease and paint the edge with egg white, then fold the petal around the paste on the end of the wire, with the pointed end of the petal at the base.

Left to right: cutters 'A', 'B' and 'C'

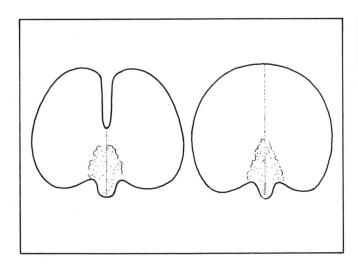

Making second and third petals: cut out shape 'B', ball and thin edges, mark centre with a crease and paint base with egg white. Place behind first petal and pinch in position. Repeat to make shape 'C' and place it behind the second petal.

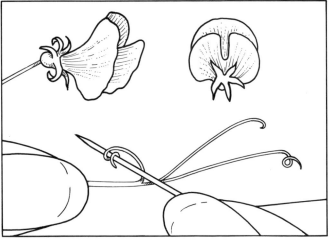

Shaping third petal and curving tendrils: when third petal is in position, take top of petal where crease is and pull back firmly. To curve the tendrils, tape the three wires together. Curve the ends round a cocktail stick (toothpick).

Thistle

Thistles take very little flower paste, are easy to make and look very attractive in an arrangement for a cake decoration.

YOU WILL NEED

Thin cardboard
Needle and mauve thread
24, 26 and 30 gauge green wire
1 length (15-20 cm/6-8 in) rose wire
Deep mauve, pink pale green and darker green dusting powders
Small pot for dusting powder
Green and pale green flower paste
Razor blade
White tape

1 Cut out two cardboard circles about 5 cm (2 in) in diameter and make a small hole in the centre of each. Put one circle on top of the other, then with a needle and the mauve thread, wind round the cardboard (see Making the stamens).

2 Cut between the two circles and securely tie round the middle with thread, then cut a 10 cm (4

in) length of 30 gauge wire and tie this round, twisting and pulling the wire down on either side of the cardboard. Cut a 7.5 cm (3 in) length of 24 gauge wire and tape it to the 30 gauge wire. Remove the cardboard.

3 Push all the threads upwards and bind the rose wire round the base until firm, and twist remaining wire round the other wires. Wind tape round to cover them.

4 Mix some mauve and pink dusting powder in small pot, then twirl the threads in this.

5 To make the calyx, take a piece of green paste and form into a rounded cone shape. Partially hollow out the narrow end with a cocktail stick (toothpick), paint the inside with egg white, then slide the calyx up the wire to position it just above the rose wire (see Making a calyx). Take off any surplus paste at the base if necessary.

6 Hold the thistle upside down and cut 'V' shapes all over the calyx with very fine scissors, then nick in the same direction with a razor blade so that the whole surface is roughened. Pull out several of the 'V' shapes with the sharp point of a cocktail stick (toothpick).

7 Take a piece of white tape twice the length of the stem and cut out an irregular shape to pro-

Making the stamens: put one cardboard circle on top of the other, then with a needle and mauve thread, wind round the cardboard until it is fairly well covered in thread. Cut between two circles and securely tie round middle with thread.

duce the thorned effect. Paint with egg white, cut in half and stick on either side of the stem. You need to press together well as it can be difficult to get this to stick. When dry, dust with pale green dusting powder.

8 To make the leaves, cut out several 7.5 cm (3 in) lengths of 26 gauge green wire (one for each leaf you want to make). Form some pale green paste into as many sausage shapes as you have lengths of wire. Dip each length of wire in a little egg

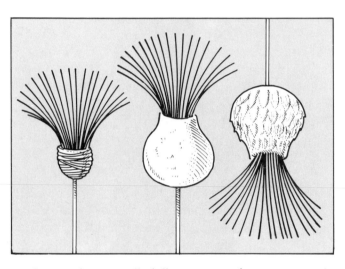

Making a calyx: partially hollow out cone of green paste, paint inside with egg white and slide calyx up wire to position it just above rose wire. Hold thistle upside down and cut 'V' shapes all over calyx, then nick with a razor blade.

white and then pull it through one of the sausage shapes of paste.

9 Roll out each piece of paste on either side of the wire until it is very thin. Then, starting from the top, cut out the leaf shape. If you are right-handed, cut out the right hand side first, then turn the leaf over and cut the other side. Make sure the points look nice and sharp. Try to bend the leaf slightly, then allow to dry.

10 When the leaves are dry, paint a little darker green colour out from the centre using light strokes, but don't take colour right to the edge.

■ There is a tremendous difference in size and colour, from the little common variety to the magnificent deep-coloured Scottish thistle, as much a part of Scotland as heather. Like fuchsia, the thistle shape lends itself to design and can be simplified in shape to use for lace, brush embroidery or simple piping. The thistle became the national emblem of Scotland in the 16th Century, fashioned from the shape of the spear thistle. It would be almost impossible to copy this plant in every detail, so it is enough to try and catch the character in the colour of the flower head and in the spiny effect on the leaves and stem.

Thistles have different meanings – the common thistle represents 'Austerity' and the Scottish thistle represents 'Retaliation'.

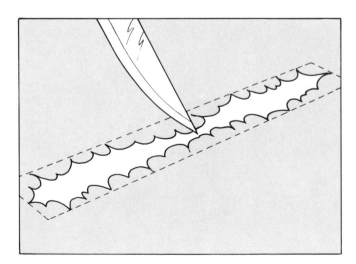

Making the thorns: take a piece of white tape twice the length of stem and cut out an irregular shape to produce the thorned effect. Paint with egg white, cut in half and stick on either side of the stem. Press well together.

Making the leaves: pull wires through sausage shapes of paste, then roll out each piece on either side of wire until thin. Starting from top, cut out leaf shape. If right-handed, cut out right first, then turn leaf over and cut the other side.

three close together, then one either side of the first three. The three cuts give you the two top petals, the two either side are the slightly larger side petals, and the bottom one is the largest of all the petals.

3 Holding the pointed end of the cone, splay out the petals, then work on the two smallest first. Pinch the top of each petal hard to make into points, then squeeze between finger and thumb. If elongated petals are required, roll with a cocktail stick (toothpick) firmly and quickly, then bend them backwards. Next, pinch the two side petals and roll with a cocktail stick (toothpick) (you may need to trim off the corners with scissors). Lastly, roll hard on the bottom petal to make it larger than the rest. Bend the side and bottom petals towards the front. Keep the back of the flower head in a pointed shape, rolling gently while you work on the petals.

4 Dip the hook into egg white, then push it through the flower head at an angle, so that it comes out about halfway down the throat. Pinch the paste to secure it on the wire. Push in a small yellow stamen until it is only just showing. Allow to dry completely.

5 To make the calyx, take a very small piece of green paste, form it into a ball, then make into a narrow cone. Open up the cone with a cocktail

Violet

The violet can either be made as a pulled flower (see page 10) or you can use a lobelia cutter (see page 50). The colouring may vary from white, to pale blue, through to deep mauve.

YOU WILL NEED

26 gauge pale green wire
White, pale blue or mauve and green flower paste
Wood dowling
Small yellow stamen
White concentrated liquid colouring
Lobelia cutter (optional)

1 To make as a pulled flower, cut a 7.5 cm (3 in) length of 26 gauge wire and make a small hook at one end. Form a small, pea-sized ball of paste into a cone shape, making sure the one end is completely flat, then push the flat end onto a piece of wood dowling to open it up, rolling it against the side of your finger so the paste is not too thick.

2 Remove it from the wood dowling and, using scissors, make five cuts in the opened-up end,

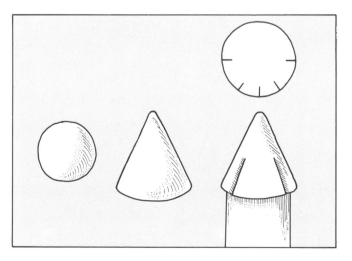

Making violet as a pulled flower: *push flat end of cone of paste onto a piece of wood dowling, rolling it against side of your finger to thin. Remove from dowling and make five cuts, three close together, then one either side of first three.*

stick (toothpick), roll the edges hard against your index finger and cut out five 'V' shapes, re-roll, then paint the inside with a little egg white. Carefully slide the calyx down the wire onto the back of the flower. Finally, shape the wire into a gentle curve.

6 If coloured paste has been used, when the flower is dry, paint inside the throat with a little white colouring to mask out the colour.

7 If making the violet with a lobelia cutter, break off a small piece of paste and form it into a cone, then into a Mexican hat shape (see page 10). Roll out very thinly and make sure the centre column is extremely thin and only about 5 mm (¼ in) high. Press the cutter onto the paste and push the flower out from the cutter with the blunt end of a cocktail stick (toothpick). Place it back on a board and cut the top petal in half.

8 Turn over and holding the flower in your left hand, open up the throat with the pointed end of a cocktail stick (toothpick). Using the blunt end, gently press from centre against each petal.

9 Work all the petals against the index finger of your left hand. Start on two top petals, rolling with the cocktail stick (toothpick) and bending them back. Then roll two side petals and, lastly, really work on the bottom largest petal in order

to make it much larger than the other petals. Curve these three petals inwards. From this stage on, the flower can be finished as for the pulled flower.

■ Together with the primrose, daffodil and cowslip, the violet is a great heralder of spring. The more familiar sweet violet is the best one to try and copy as it conjures up a wonderful scent, and the colour is deeper than the other varieties. Don't worry too much over the precise colour of this flower as there are so many different kinds. Look carefully at the different shapes and colours of the leaves because, as with so many plants, the green offsets the colour of the flowers.

The violet has been used for many years as a decorative addition to cooking, eithered sugared (painted with egg white and then dipped in sugar) or used in flavourings.

As this flower can be difficult to copy, it is possibly best first made in white paste; once the colour is added to the paste it can make it a little more difficult to work, especially when working on a small scale.

If you are interested in completing more details on this plant, you will notice a tiny green structure a little way down the stem from the flower head. This can be achieved by cutting the flower tape to half width, about 5 mm (¼ in) in length. Cut out a wide 'V' shape and bind round wire, then adjust points with tweezers.

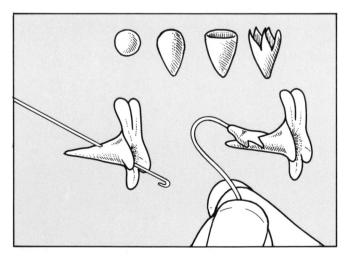

Making the calyx: *open up the cone of green paste, roll edges hard against your index finger and cut out five 'V' shapes. Re-roll, then paint the inside with egg white. Carefully slide the calyx down the wire onto the back of the flower.*

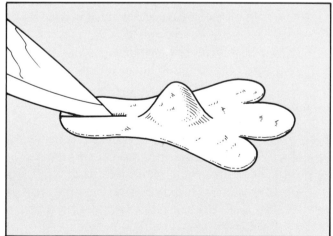

Cutting violet with a lobelia cutter: *form cone of paste into a Mexican hat shape, roll out very thinly, making sure centre column is extremely thin. Press cutter onto paste and cut out. Place shape on board and cut top petal in half.*

Wild Rose

This delicate flower is best displayed in an arrangement with lots of leaves and the flowers in all different stages, from the tight buds through to the stage when the petals have fallen.

YOU WILL NEED

24, 28 and 30 gauge green wire
Cream thread
Green tape
Light green, dark green and white flower paste
Yellow, brown and pink dusting powder
Primrose, snowdrop and calyx cutters as shown
Fine needle

---

1 Cut a 10 cm (4 in) length of 30 gauge wire, place alongside your finger, then wind the thread round both finger and wire many times. Slide the thread off your finger, pull down the wire either side of the loop of threads and then twist the two pieces of wire together tightly (see Making the stamens).

2 Tie a piece of thread around the loop of threads just above where the wire goes through and secure with knots. Tape this 30 gauge wire to a 10

cm (4 in) length of 24 gauge wire, and then wind a little tape securely round the base of the thread. Snip through the loop of threads and cut the stamens to the required length. Separate the threads in the centre with the end of a paint brush, leaving a small space.

3 Paint the centre with a little egg white, then drop in a tiny ball of light green paste. With two fingers and thumb, press it into shape.

4 Holding the threads firmly, paint the ends with egg white, then dip into yellow dusting powder to form pollen. To make older flowers, use a darker cream thread for the stamens, and dip into brown dusting powder.

5 Place a thick piece of white paste on a board and roll out until very thin, but leaving a raised part in the middle. Place a primrose cutter over the raised part and cut out the shape.

6 Put the shape on your hand and soften the edges with a balling tool. Turn the paste over so the raised part is uppermost, then gently thin the edges by applying pressure with a cocktail stick (toothpick). You may need to re-cut the heart shape petals with scissors at this stage.

7 Place the flower on a piece of foam and curve the petals inwards using a balling tool.

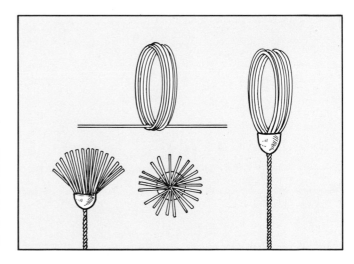

Making the stamens: slide loop of thread off your finger, pull wire down either side and twist two pieces together tightly. Tie piece of thread round loop and secure. Wind tape round base of thread, snip loop and cut stamens, then separate.

8 Paint a little egg white onto the wire stem below the stamens. Pull the wire through the flower shape until the petals are positioned around the stamens. Allow to dry.

9 Using pink dusting powder, carefully colour the petals, adding more colour to outer edge of each of the petals. Dust the back of the petals.

10 When all the flowers have been made, roll out two quantities of light and dark green paste. (Keep some of the darker paste on one side). Put one colour on top of the other and roll, pressing hard, then cut out calyx shapes. Working on one at a time and keeping the others well covered, thin down the edges either with a balling tool or cocktail stick (toothpick). Make small cuts at the edges to feather them. Place the calyx on a piece of foam, light green sides uppermost, and cup with a balling tool. Paint the centre with egg white, then slide it up one of the wires and position directly behind the flower head, with the darker green underneath.

11 Take a tiny piece of the reserved darker paste and roll into a ball. Paint an area with egg white, then thread the wire through it to position the painted part directly below the calyx.

12 To make a bud, shape a small cone of paste just under 1 cm (½ in) long on a 10 cm (4 in)

length of 24 gauge wire and allow to dry overnight. Roll out some white paste, cut out a snowdrop shape with the cutter, and thin the edges. Paint the cone with egg white, then slide the petals up the wire and wrap them around the cone. When dry, brush with darker pink dusting powder than used on the open flowers. Make the calyx as before, but close the sepals around the bud.

13 To make leaves, form some green paste into a sausage shape. Cut a 10 cm (4 in) length of 28 gauge wire and dip in egg white, then pull it through the paste. With a paint brush handle or something similar, roll out the paste either side of the wire. Using a palette knife, lift it onto your hand and thin the edges with a balling tool until very thin. Cut out a leaf shape.

14 Repeat to make five leaves, making one bigger leaf for the end. When forming each leaf, place it on a board and break the edge with a needle to create a serrated edge. Tape the wire holding the leaves to the wire of the flower.

Left to right: primrose, snowdrop and calyx cutters

Shaping the petals: cut out primrose shape and soften edges with a balling tool, then with raised part uppermost, gently thin edges with a cocktail stick (toothpick). Place flower on a piece of foam and curve petals inwards using balling tool.

Making the calyx: cut calyx shapes, thin edges with balling tool or cocktail stick (toothpick), then make small cuts at edges to feather them. Place on foam, light green sides uppermost, and cup. Paint with egg white, then fix behind flower head.

Winter Jasmine

This is a lovely flower to include in an arrangement with a winter theme for either a man's or a woman's cake. Add some small twigs with different coloured berries and leaves.

YOU WILL NEED

24, and 28 gauge green wire
Yellow and green flower paste
Wood dowling
Very pale green stamen
Gum arabic solution (see page 110), egg white or confectioners' glaze
Yellow and gold or silver dusting powder
Brown colouring
Green tape

1 Cut a 7.5 cm (3 in) length of 24 gauge wire and make a hook at one end. Shape a long thin cone of yellow paste, push onto a piece of wood dowling, and make six short cuts. Make sure paste is thin at this point by carefully moulding it round the piece of wood dowling.

2 Take the paste off the dowling and spread out the petals. Pinch the petal ends together, then roll each petal with a cocktail stick (toothpick) against your index finger, then put some movement into the petals.

3 Roll the back of the flower throat until it is narrow. Dip the hooked wire in egg white and pass it through the throat of the flower. Put the pale green stamen in place. Allow to dry.

4 When dry, paint the back of the flower only with gum arabic solution, egg white or confectioners' glaze. Brush the flower with yellow and gold or silver dusting powder.

5 Paint very small amounts of brown colouring on the throat of the flower.

6 To make the calyx, make a long, thin sausage shape of green paste and open up one end with the pointed end of a cocktail stick (toothpick). Cut out six 'V' shapes and re-roll in order to make the paste very fine. Repeat with a smaller amount of paste to make a tiny calyx, but with only four sepals, to fit over the base of the larger one.

7 Either paint on small brown bud coverings at the base of the second calyx, or stick on two tiny pieces of brown paste.

8 Buds vary in size from the very small green to large yellow ones.

Making the calyx: *make a thin sausage of green paste and open up one end. Cut out six 'V' shapes and re-roll to make paste very fine. Repeat with smaller amount of paste to make a tiny calyx with four sepals, to fit over base of larger one.*

⌒◦⊷ ALSTROEMERIA CAKE ⊶◦⌒

The lovely trumpet-shaped alstroemeria flowers (see page 12) in subtle shades of pinks, oranges and yellow and white with long slender leaves make an unusual and very attractive arrangement for a special occasion cake. The simple design is completed with a lacy frill and a pretty trail of icing dots around the base of the cake.

■ To make these celebration cakes look extra special, the cake boards can be covered with sugarpaste to match the cakes. Cover a cake board in exactly the same way as a cake (see page 110). Roll out the sugarpaste on a lightly sugared work surface. Slide the rolling pin under the paste, lift it up and place on the cake board. Dust your hands with cornflour (cornstarch) and rotate the palm of your hand on the top to smooth the paste and expel any air. Smooth the surface of the paste with a cake smoother to remove any creases or blemishes. Fix a ribbon around the edge of the cake board.

■ Arrange the spray of flowers and leaves in a plastic container and push it into the top of the cake. Make up some royal icing (see page 108) and put into a piping (pastry) bag fitted with a size 0 plain writing tube (nozzle) and pipe dots around the base of the cake (this is known as a snail's trail). Pipe another snail's trail in the shape of an alstroemeria leaf on top of cake.

■ For the side of the cake, make and attach a royal icing lacework frill (see pages 108 and 109) while white lace is still attached to board, dust with green and pink powder colours (or colours of choice).

❧ BLUEBELL CAKE ❧

This delightful springtime cake has an arrangement of primroses (see page 62) and cowslips (see page 28) on the top and bluebells (see page 17) set in pebbles (see page 99) around the side. The side of the cake is also decorated with a countryside scene of hills, trees, hedges and houses.

■ Arrange the primroses and cowslips in two plastic containers and push into the top of the cake.

■ To make the scene on the side of the cake, roll out pale violet paste and cut out the shapes of the distant hills. Fix onto the cake with egg white.

■ The trees can be made with the cutters of your choice from the ones used to make the flowers; for instance, here the oak leaf cutter and the orchid cutter are used to make the tall trees, the anemone leaf for the lower trees – the edges are broken with a cocktail stick (toothpick). Half a large blossom cutter is

used to make the hedges and, again, the edges are broken with a cocktail stick (toothpick).

■ Cut out the shapes for the farmhouse and church from brown and white or cream paste. Cut out shapes from green paste for the cake board to give the impression of green fields. Press white and yellow non-pareils (tiny pellets of paste) into this paste to look like flowers.

■ Arrange one or more groups of bluebells in one or more pieces of paste and arrange on the cake board. Paint the piece(s) of paste with royal icing and immediately stick on the pebbles.

This cake has an arrangement of buttercups (see page 19), ivy-leaved toadflax (see page 44) and plantains (see page 58) set in pebbles on the top. The side of the cake is decorated with a single frill of ivy leaves and deeper frills made from green and white paste cut out and shaped like anemone leaves. Tiny gelatine droplets (see page 110) are stuck onto the frills with royal icing (see page 108).

■ Arrange the buttercups, ivy-leaved toadflax and plantains in a plastic container and push it into the cake. Arrange a pile of pebbles around the base of the arrangement.

■ To make the deeper frills for the side of the cake, roll out green and white paste, rolling it flatter than when making leaves on a wire and cut out anemone leaves, using the cutter shown on page 15 and cutting the leaves as instructed. Using the shaper template illustrated on page 109, mark where you want the leaves to go on the side of the cake, then dab royal icing on the back of each leaf and stick onto the cake.

■ To make the ivy leaves, roll out one 10 cm (4 in) x 1 cm (½ in) strip of green paste at a time. Press the back of an ivy-leaved toadflax all the way along the length of the strip. Cut off one leaf and cover the rest while you cut out the first one with scissors. Mark the veins and colour the leaf, if wished. Stick the leaf onto the cake with royal icing. Repeat to make enough leaves to go all the way round the cake, making slightly larger leaves for the top of the curves.

■ When all the leaves have dried, stick on gelatine droplets with a tiny amount of royal icing.

❧ CHRYSANTHEMUM CAKE ❧

This simple round cake is stunningly decorated with chrysanthemums (see page 23) and leaves (see pages 100 – 103) in beautiful autumnal shades of browns, oranges and greens, with a royal icing lacework frill (see page 108 and 109) around the side and a snail's trail of tiny dots made from royal icing around the base.

■ Arrange the chrysanthemums and leaves for the central decoration on the top of the cake in a plastic container and push the container into the cake. Stick on extra leaves made without any wires with a dab of royal icing.

■ Make some royal icing (see page 108) and put in a piping (pastry) bag fitted with a size 0 plain writing tube (nozzle), then pipe a snail's trail of icing dots around base of cake.

■ The side of cake is decorated with picot edging, done by piping three dots of royal icing, then two, then one (see photograph). Push a gelatine droplet (see page 110) into the single dot while the icing is still soft. Use the shaper template illustrated on page 109 to mark the position before starting to pipe the edging.

■ Arrange halved chrysanthemums and leaves on the cake board around the cake and pipe more icing dots between the leaves.

This cake has been baked in a bell-shaped tin (pan), which is available from specialist cake shops, but the decoration of different coloured cornflowers (see page 26) and trailing lobelia (see page 50) could be used on any shape cake.

■ Make up some royal icing (see page 108) and use to pipe a pretty trailing design of your choice on the side of the cake, such as the leaf - and flower-like design with dots used here (ideally it should follow the trailing design of your flower arrangement).

■ Make a royal icing lacework frill (see pages 108 and 109) and attach it all around the side of the cake with royal icing. Pipe small royal icing dots all round the base of the cake. Allow to dry completely before

positioning the flowers on the top of the cake and the sprays around the base of the cake.

■ Arrange the flowers for the top of the cake in a plastic container and push it into the cake. On the cake board around the cake, arrange pretty sprays, each one made up of five lobelia flowers, a single cornflower and a white ribbon bow attached to the spray's stem. Secure these sprays to the cake board with a little royal icing.

This pretty petal-shaped cake is very easy to decorate. The arrangement of pink cyclamen flowers (see page 30) on the top of the cake is placed in several flower containers which are set in a scattering of white pebbles (see page 99), and the side of the cake is decorated with a frill of cyclamen petals and hearts.

■ To make the three-coloured petal frill for the side of the cake, roll out a dark and a light shade of pink paste and also some white paste, then cut out lots of petals using the cutter that is used to make the cyclamen petals for the flowers (see page 31).

■ Work on one petal at a time, keeping the rest well covered to prevent them drying out. Thin down each petal and stick it onto the cake with a little royal icing, using the shaper template illustrated on page 109 to help you position them in a curved frill on the cake.

■ Place the petal at the highest point of each loop of the curve in position last.

■ Roll out some white paste and cut out enough heart shapes to go all the way round the cake. Stick them in position in the same way as the petal frill, following the same curves as the lower frill.

DAFFODIL CAKE

Little groups of daffodils (see page 32) and narcissi (see page 51) with their leaves are arranged on the top of this cake and surrounded by white and green pebbles. More flowers are clustered in a pile of pebbles on the cake board at one corner of the cake and oak leaves are scattered across the cake and cake board. A frill of flowers, piped dots, yellow non-pareils and lichen complete the design.

■ Yellow non-pareils (tiny pellets of paste) are kneaded into the sugar-paste covering cake and pressed into the paste on the cake board. Arrange the daffodils and narcissi for the top of the cake in three different containers and sink them into the cake. Surround the tops of the containers with pebbles.

■ Make up some royal icing (see page 108) and put into a piping (pastry) bag fitted with a size 0 plain writing tube (nozzle) and pipe a snail's trail of tiny dots around the base of the cake and a few little dots by the flowers on the top of the cake.

■ To make the lichen, roll out some pale green paste, cut out with a blossom cutter, cut in half, then thin the edges and press with a balling tool to cup. Dust with green dusting powder when dry.

■ To make the frill of daffodil and narcissi heads, make the flowers in the usual way but without the stamens and wires. Allow to dry and then fix them onto the cake with royal icing.

■ Arrange a group of flowers and leaves in a piece of paste at one corner of the cake. Paint the piece of paste with royal icing, a small area at a time, and stick on pebbles.

～ DAISY CAKE ～

An arrangement of clover (see page 24), clover leaves and a single daisy (see page 33) are set in a shallow pile of pebbles (see page 99) on the top of this cake and the side of the cake is decorated with a honeycomb design in two shades or orange and yellow. A single daisy set in a pile of white and cream pebbles is positioned at each corner of the hexagonal shape of the cake.

■ Arrange the clover, leaves and daisy for the top of the cake in a plastic container and push it into the cake. Surround the top of the container (the base of the flower arrangement) with a few white and cream pebbles.

■ Make some royal icing (see page 108) and put in a piping (pastry) bag fitted with a size 0 plain writing tube (nozzle), then pipe a snail's trail of icing dots around the side of the cake, about 2.5 cm (1 in) down from the top and around the base of the cake. Pipe several trails of dots on the top of the cake.

■ Between the two snail's trails of

dots on the side of the cake, mark a six-sided honeycomb design (either draw it freehand or if you can find a suitable cutter the right shape, lightly mark the sugarpaste covering on the cake). Colour in each of the hexagons with orange and yellow concentrated liquid colouring, using a very fine paintbrush.

■ Arrange a single daisy in each of six pieces of paste and position at each corner of the cake. Paint the pieces of paste with royal icing, one at a time, and immediately stick on white and cream pebbles. Pipe a few more royal icing dots at random around pebbles on the cake board.

⊷ FUCHSIA CAKE ⊶

Bright pink fuchsia flowers (see page 36) make a stunning decoration for this cake and the colour theme continues on the side of the cake with flat fuchsia flowers stuck onto the sugarpaste covering. A snail's trail of royal icing dots (see page 108) around the base of the cake completes the design.

■ Arrange the fuchsia flowers in a plastic container and push it into the centre of the cake.
■ Make some royal icing and put it into a piping (pastry) bag fitted with a size 0 plain writing tube (nozzle), then pipe tiny dots around the base of the cake.
■ To make the design for the side of the cake, cut out two petals for each shape, using a rose petal cutter. Allow the petals to dry, then dust them with deep mauve dusting powder.
■ Put some pink royal icing in a pip-

ing (pastry) bag and pipe a pistil and stamens for each flower shape, then stick the dry petals onto the cake with royal icing, placing one partly behind the other.
■ For the outer petals, cut out the shapes shown on page 36 (see Making the decoration for the side of the fuchsia cake and Assembling design on the side of the cake). Stick onto the cake with royal icing. Draw the leaves freehand. Pipe a thick edge to the leaf, then pull the icing down with a wet paintbrush (this is called brush embroidery).

This attractive cake is a lovely mixture of autumnal colours – the rich reddish browns and pinks of the spindle berries (see page 67), the muted browns and greens of the hazelnuts (see page 39) and the delicate silver and brown of the honesty (see page 41). The subtle colours of the top of the cake are offset by the strong, toning reds and greens of the leafy frill around the side of the cake.

■ Arrange the honesty, spindle berries and hazelnuts in plastic containers and push them into the centre of the cake.
■ To make the leaf frill around the side of the cake, roll out red and green paste and cut out the leaf shapes. Working on a few at a time, and keeping the rest well covered to prevent them drying out, press the leaves into leaf moulds to mark the veins on them, then fix them onto the cake with a little dab of royal icing (see page 108) before they dry.

Use the shaper template shown on page 109 to help you mark the curve around the cake before positioning the leaves.
■ Put some royal icing in a piping (pastry) bag fitted with a size 0 plain writing tube (nozzle) and pipe a dot of white icing in the centre of the ivy leaves on the top row of the curved fringe and another on the pointed end of each of the green leaves in the central row. Pipe more dots on the side of the cake above the fringe.

‏❧ JAPONICA CAKE ‏❧

Delicate japonica flowers (see page 46) on their twigs are arranged on the top of this cake. As the japonica originally came from China and Japan, the side of the cake is decorated with a Chinese dragon painted on the paste. A ribbon secured around the side of the cake below the dragon, and a snail's trail of tiny royal icing dots piped around the base complete the design. See page 47 for the dragon template.

■ To make the dragon for the side of the cake, trace the template onto tracing paper, then prick the outline of the template onto the sugarpaste on the side of the cake. Either paint the design shown here, or devise your own dragon design, and paint on with concentrated liquid colourings. Allow the painted dragon to dry before completing the cake decoration.

■ Make up some royal icing (see page 108) and put into a piping (pastry) bag fitted with a size 0 plain writing tube (nozzle), then pipe a snail's trail of tiny dots all around the base of the cake.

■ Fix the ribbon onto side of the cake with royal icing (see page 108). Overlap the ends of the ribbon 5 mm (¼ in) and secure with two pins either side of the overlap to secure one end to the other and to the cake. Cut a 10 cm (4 in) piece of ribbon and tie a granny knot in the middle so that you have a bow shape, then cut a 'V' in the ends. Put a dot of icing on the overlap on the ribbon on the cake and press this bow on. Remove excess icing, leave to dry then remove pins.

■ Arrange the japonica in a plastic container together with ribbon bows, then sink container into cake.

❦ NASTURTIUM CAKE ❦

This lovely heart-shaped cake is decorated with colourful nasturtium flowers and trailing leaves of different sizes (see page 53). More trailing leaves decorate the side of the cake and a snail's trail of icing dots around the base of the cake completes the design.

■ Arrange the nasturtium flowers and leaves for the top of the cake in a plastic container and push it into the cake.

■ Make up some royal icing (see page 108) and put in a piping (pastry) bag fitted with a size 0 plain writing tube (nozzle), then pipe a snail's trail of tiny icing dots around the base of the cake.

■ For the side of the cake you need to make graded sizes of nasturtium leaves following the instructions on page 53, making several of each

size. Allow to dry.

■ At each place you want a leaf to be attached on the side of the cake, make a slit in the icing the width of the leaf. These slits must be made within a day of covering the cake with the sugarpaste or it will have dried and be too hard.

■ Paint the underside of each leaf with egg white and then push it into the slit at an angle. Pipe royal icing dots and veins on the leaves and a looping trail from one leaf to the next in each set of graded leaves.

❧ POPPY CAKE ❧

This cake is decorated with poppies (see page 61) and honeysuckle (see page 42) with a snail's trail of tiny dots around the base. Poppy leaves are too fragile to be able to make them successfully in flower paste, so grasses made of ribbon are used here.

■ To make the ribbon grasses used for the arrangement on this cake, you need lengths of ribbon which reflect the colours of summer grasses, such as cream, mid-green and pale green.

■ Cut the ribbon into 15 cm (6 in) lengths. Place the ribbons side by side horizontally, then place a length of 28 gauge green wire across them vertically.

■ Holding the ends of the ribbons, pull them upwards and the wire down to loop it over the ribbon. Twist the wires together. Tie rose wire round the ribbons just above the loop of wire. Cut each ribbon

down through the middle, then taper the ends. Run a flat-bladed knife up the ribbon to curl it.

■ Cut out a fluted shape of sugarpaste and place on cake. Pipe dots around edge. Arrange flowers in plastic containers and push into the cake through the shape.

■ Make some royal icing (see page 108) and put in a piping (pastry) bag fitted with a size 0 plain writing tube (nozzle), then pipe a snail's trail of tiny icing dots around the base of the cake. Pipe more dots from the top of the cake down the sides.

■ Arrange flowers and leaves around the sides of the cake.

❧ SNOWDROP CAKE ❧

The top of this cake is decorated with a spray of snowdrops (see page 66) with some white pebbles (see page 99) and a snail's trail of tiny dots made from royal icing (see page 108). The side of the cake is decorated with a fringe of white leaves and violets (see page 73) set in pebbles, and fan-shaped pieces set in the side.

■ To make the green fan-shaped pieces on the side of the cake, cut out a template to make an inverted 'V' shape. Roll out a piece of green paste fairly thinly, then cut out the 'V' shape using template.

■ Paint the area of the cake where the green paste is to be positioned with egg white and stick on the green paste. Once in place, take a wooden skewer and, starting from the centre, press it into the paste to make indentations in a fan shape – to give the impression of stalks. Repeat to make four of these and position them around the cake (see photograph). Put royal icing in a

piping (pastry) bag fitted with a size 0 plain writing tube (nozzle) and pipe dots around the base.

■ Roll out some white paste and cut out lots of leaves, using a small leaf cutter. Gently shape each of the leaves from behind with a balling tool so that they are not completely flat. Fix the leaves onto the cake with royal icing, sticking them all around the base of the cake, then pipe a tiny bulb of green royal icing at the top of each one.

■ Secure the violets in a piece of flower paste. Coat the piece of paste with royal icing, a small area at a time, then stick pebbles on.

This pretty, shaped cake is covered with pale green sugarpaste, which provides a lovely contrast to the dainty white summer jasmine flowers (see page 68) in the arrangement on the top and around the sides of the cake.

■ The flowers for the decoration on the side of this cake must be placed in position on the cake before the sugarpaste covering has dried. Make the jasmine flowers for the side of the cake without any wires and push them straight into the sugarpaste – this way they are completely edible.

■ Push groups of other summer jasmine flowers made without wires into the still-soft sugarpaste on the cake board.

■ Arrange the summer jasmine flowers for the top of the cake in a plastic container and push the container into the centre of the cake.

■ Make up some royal icing (see page 108) and put it in a piping (pastry) bag fitted with a size 0 plain writing nozzle, then pipe a snail's trail of tiny icing dots all around the base of the cake. Pipe more dots around the flowers on the side of the cake and a few beside the flowers on the cake board.

⚘ SWEET PEA CAKE ⚘

All the colour for this delightful summery cake is provided by the sweet peas (see page 69) and their delicate trailing tendrils, so the sides of the cake have been kept very simple – just plain ribbons picking up some of the lovely sweet pea colours.

■ Arrange a selection of different coloured sweet peas in a plastic container and push it into the centre of the cake. Bend some of the tendrils so that they trail over the top of the cake and down the sides.
■ Make up some royal icing (see page 108) and put in a piping (pastry) bag fitted with a size 0 plain writing tube (nozzle), then pipe a snail's trail of tiny icing dots around the base of the cake.
■ Just above the snail's trail, fix two different coloured ribbons with royal icing (use coloured ribbons

that tone with the sweet peas used in the flower arrangement). Overlap the ends of the ribbon 5 mm (¼ in) and secure with two pins either side of the overlap to secure one end to the other and to the cake.
■ Cut a 10 cm (4 in) piece of ribbon and tie a granny knot in the middle so that you have a bow shape, then cut a 'V' in each of the ends. Put a dot of icing on the overlap on the ribbon on the cake and press this bow onto it. Carefully remove any excess royal icing. Leave it to dry, then remove the pins.

❧ THISTLE CAKE ❧

The top of the cake is decorated with thistles (see page 71) and a tartan scarf made from flower paste. Each corner of the cake is covered with a Scottish jabot (lacy cloth worn at the throat). The sides of the cake are decorated with a royal icing lacework frill (see pages 108 and 109) and the base with small dots. Sprigs of heather (see page 40) are placed on the cake board.

■ Roll out some white paste and cut out a scarf shape. Allow to dry. Colour it, either following the design shown here or making your own design. Arrange on the top of the cake. Arrange the thistles in a plastic container and push it into the top of the cake.

■ To make a jabot, cut out a semi-circle template slightly less deep than the depth of the cake. Cut a smaller triangle that will fit inside the semi-circle. Mix together some white sugarpaste and flower paste and roll out fairly thinly. Put the template on the paste and cut round it.

■ Place the triangle on the paste to mark lightly where the creases should go, then pleat the edge part either side. Trim off the excess paste at the point. Repeat to make four jabots. Fix a lacework frill all the way round each jabot.

■ Make up some royal icing (see page 108) and put into a piping (pastry) bag fitted with a size 0 plain writing tube (nozzle) and pipe a snail's trail around base of cake.

■ Fit a jabot onto each corner of the cake with royal icing. Place a royal icing lacework frill on each side of the cake. Arrange some heather on the cake board.

✺ WILD ROSE CAKE ✺

This cake has an arrangement of wild roses (see page 75) set in white and cream pebbles (see page 99) on the top, with sprays of wild roses and toadstools (see page 99) around the sides. Royal icing lacework (see pages 108 and 109) and a snail's trail of icing dots complete the decoration.

■ Arrange the flowers for the top of the cake in a plastic container and push it into the cake. Secure the base of the arrangement with a large piece of flower paste, paint the paste with royal icing (see page 108), a small area at a time and immediately stick the white and cream pebbles onto the icing before it dries.

■ Make some royal icing and put in a piping (pastry) bag fitted with a size 0 plain writing tube (nozzle), then pipe a snail's trail of tiny dots around the base of the cake and a few small trails of dots on the top of the cake.

■ To position the royal icing lacework on side of the cake, pipe seven dots at a time, fix one of the laceworks onto the dots, then pipe the next seven dots and fix on the next lacework, continue round the cake, leaving gaps where you are going to position the flowers and toadstools on the cake board.

■ Secure the toadstools and sprays of flowers in pieces of flower paste and place them in position on the cake board. Paint each piece of paste with royal icing and stick on more cream and white pebbles. Pipe on small dots around pebbles on the cake board. Leave to dry.

∽ WINTER JASMINE CAKE ∽

This pretty wintertime cake has a lovely arrangement of delicate yellow winter jasmine flowers (see page 77), trailing ivy leaves (see pages 100 and 103) and larch fir cones (see page 48). As the ivy trails down over the sides of the cake, the rest of the design on the side is very simple, just a snail's trail of dots around the base and two ribbons tied just above the dots.

■ Arrange the winter jasmine flowers, long stems of ivy and larch fir cones in a plastic container and push it into the centre of the cake. Spread out the ivy so that the leaves trail down over the sides of the cake.

■ Make some royal icing (see page 108) and put in a piping (pastry) bag fitted with a size 0 plain writing tube (nozzle), then pipe a snail's trail of tiny icing dots all around the base of the cake.

■ Fix one ribbon at a time onto the side of the cake with royal icing. Overlap the ends of the ribbon 5 mm (¼ in) and secure with two pins either side of the overlap to secure one end to the other and to the cake. Cut a 10 cm (4 in) piece of ribbon and tie a granny knot in the middle so that you have a bow shape, then cut a 'V' in the ends. Put a dot of icing on the overlap on the ribbon on the cake and press this bow onto it. Remove any excess royal icing, leave to dry and then remove the pins.

Spring and summer are represented on this beautiful wedding cake. The top layer has narcissi (see page 51), violets (see page 73) and snowdrops (see page 66) set in white pebbles (see page 99), with roses (see page 64) and gypsophila (see page 38) on the top and around side.

The second layer is decorated with nasturtiums (see page 52), sweet peas (see page 69) and honeysuckle (see page 42) set in peach-coloured pebbles, with roses and gypsophila around side.

■ For the top of the cake arrange the roses and gypsophila in a plastic container and push it into the cake. Around the side of the top tier of the cake, arrange the spring flowers — the narcissi, violets and snowdrops set in white pebbles, with roses and gyposphila in every other section.

■ For the bottom tier, arrange the summer flowers — nasturtiums, sweet peas and honeysuckle, this time set in peach-coloured pebbles, again with roses and gypsophilia in every other section.

■ Make some royal icing (see page 108) and put in a piping (pastry) bag fitted with a size 0 plain writing tube (nozzle), then pipe a snail's trail of tiny icing dots around the top and the base of each cake.

■ Mark the different sections on each layer of the cake with a royal icing lacework frill (see pages 108 and 109 for making and attaching the frill).

■ To make the heart-shaped cut-out on the bottom layer, cut out a heart-shape template the size you require. Roll out some white flower paste and cut out the heart, using the template. Pipe a picot edging of royal icing around the edge and the initials of the couple in the centre. Rest the heart on a roll of paste.

ADDITIONAL
DECORATIONS

As well as all the different flowers shown on the previous pages, there are all sorts of other attractive decorations that you can make and incorporate in your arrangements for celebration cakes. In this chapter you will find ideas for additional decorations plus templates for many different leaf shapes.

Life-like pebbles, toadstools, twigs and many different varieties of leaves can be made from flower paste and then coloured and shaded in the same way as the flowers in this book. They all add interest to the decoration and help to make your design look extra special.

Pebbles, in particular, which only take a few seconds to make, are a very effective way of hiding the top of the container holding the flower arrangement when it is pushed into the cake. They can also be used for decorations around the side of the cake. Flowers can be arranged in a lump of flower paste and stuck onto the cake board. The lump of paste can then be painted with royal icing and pebbles stuck onto it before the icing dries. The flowers then look as if they are arranged in a pile of pebbles.

Twigs are essential for flowers like japonica (see page 46) and the Japonica cake (see page 88). They look very attractive and help to make arrangements look more natural. They are easy to make, needing only brown wire and florists' stretch tape.

Pebbles

Pebbles are very useful as an extra decoration for flower arrangements on cakes. There are two different methods of making them.

YOU WILL NEED

White and pale cream flower paste
Black and brown colouring, or different coloured flower paste

1 Take a lump of white paste and knead it until it is pliable. Dip cocktail sticks (toothpicks) in black and brown colouring and wipe them across the white paste. Knead again, but only slightly, then break off small pieces with your thumb nail. Drop them onto a plate and allow to dry hard (preferably overnight). They can be used straight away, but will stay soft for some time and may be crushed when being put in position.

2 Alternatively, knead different coloured pastes into a lump of white paste, then break off pieces.

3 Make quite a few pebbles in pure white or pale cream as these show up the coloured stones. Make some round and flatten others.

Toadstools

These make a very pretty decoration if they are secured in a pile of pebbles.

YOU WILL NEED

Cream or very pale yellow flower paste coloured with very small amounts of brown and black
Cream, brown and black dusting powder

1 To make the stalk, form a small sausage shape of paste and push a piece of uncooked spaghetti through the middle; set aside.

2 To make the cap, take a larger piece of paste and form into a cone. Hollow it out with a cocktail stick (toothpick) and thin down the edges with a balling tool. Mark the gills on the underside with a small knife.

3 Allow to dry, then paint centre of underneath of the cap with egg white, fix in a small piece of paste, then push in the stalk.

4 Brush with dusting powder to shade the toadstool. To make a frill on the stalk, cut a narrow strip of paste and frill it by rolling the edge with a cocktail stick (toothpick). Fix it round the stalk just below the level of the toadstool cap.

Assembling toadstools: paint centre of underneath of cap with egg white, then push in stalk. Shade with dusting powder. Cut a strip of paste, frill edge and fix round the stalk.

Twigs

It is useful to be able to make thin twigs, especially when doing more natural arrangements and flowers such as japonica. They are extremely quick to make and look very effective.

YOU WILL NEED

26 gauge brown wire
Olive green tape

1 Cut a piece of wire the length that you require for the arrangement. Cut some tape in half to halve its width, then tear off about a 1 cm (½ in) length from one end.

2 Roll the top part of the tape between your finger and thumb, then bend it over and pinch to form a bud (see Forming a bud), making sure that the bottom half is still flat.

3 Roll it onto the end of the wire to form the first bud, rolling flat part of the tape around wire.

4 Bind some more tape from underneath the top bud down the wire for about 2.5 cm (1 in), then break it off. Form another bud as described above, and attach it to the wire.

5 Keep binding more olive green tape onto the wire and adding more buds on alternate sides of the stem.

6 If you find the buds all end up on the same side of the stem when you've rolled them on, you can move them round the wire with your fingers or a pair of tweezers.

7 Make several other smaller twigs in the same way as above, and then bind these twigs onto the first stem. Any flowers or leaves needed for your decorative arrangements can be attached to the twigs as you go along.

Leaves

Notice how leaves are shaped, in what order they come on the stalk and which ones have a shiny surface. Always try to add some extra colour, either with dusting powder or with different concentrated liquid colourings.

YOU WILL NEED

26, 28 and 30 gauge green wire
An assortment of different shades of green flower paste, plus cream paste if making variegated leaves
Green concentrated liquid colouring mixed with gum arabic solution (see page 110)
White dusting powder
Colourless alcohol, such as kirsch
Blue and green concentrated liquid colouring

1 You do not have to be a botonist to be able to observe how leaves are shaped, and in what order they come on the stalk. For most leaves you can use the sausage of paste method explained here. As a general rule, if making larger leaves, cut 5 cm (2 in) lengths of 26 gauge wire; if making small leaves, cut lengths of 28 gauge wire. Longer lengths of wire are required for certain plants such as daffodil and snowdrop.

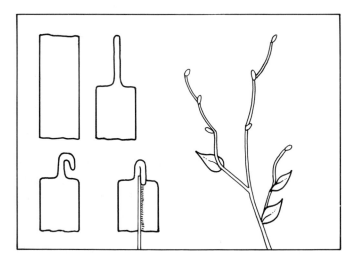

Forming a bud: cut some tape in half to halve its width, then tear off about a 1 cm (½ in) length. Roll top part of tape between your finger and thumb, then bend and pinch to form a bud. Roll it onto wire, rolling flat part of tape around wire.

2 Form some paste into a sausage shape. Dip one of the wires in egg white and pull down through the paste until about 1 cm (½ in) is still embedded in the paste.

3 Roll out the paste, very gently over the wire and more firmly either side until it is very thin. Cut to the required shape with scissors or a cutter, then press the edges of the leaves with a balling tool to give them a feeling of movement and make them seem more natural.

4 To make leaves with jagged edges, cut lengths of 28 or 30 gauge wire. Make the leaf as described above; rose petal cutters, used either way round, are very useful for cutting leaf shapes. Starting from the top of the shape, using the pointed end of a cocktail stick (toothpick), press it into the paste on the edge of the leaf and twist the cocktail stick (toothpick) slightly. Continue down to the bottom curve. Clean the stick every so often otherwise it will collect paste and spoil the clean cut.

5 Mark the veins with a sharp modelling tool, or use a leaf mould, taking care not to put too much pressure on the wire. Curve some leaves in an arrangement – it is very uninteresting to see all the leaves lying straight and flat – and allow to dry before adding extra colours and assembling the leaves on a main stalk.

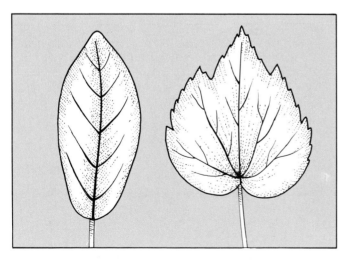

Marking the veins: paint the leaves with green colouring and gum arabic solution. Using the blunt end of a cocktail stick (toothpick), take off the paint where the veins go, wiping the cocktail stick (toothpick) clean each time you put in a vein.

6 To make more complicated shapes, make a template if the real leaf is available. Take a thin piece of cardboard and cover an area slightly larger than the leaf with double-sided tape. Press on the leaf, right side down, and cut round the edge. This will give you a template you should be able to use over and over again. It is usually easier to cut the different shapes with scissors rather than a knife. Do not make too many indentations in the lower part of the structure as this tends to weaken the leaf.

7 Paint the leaves with the green colouring mixed with gum arabic solution (the colour should be darker than the colour used to make the leaf). Don't make all the leaves exactly the same colour in an arrangement – in nature they are sometimes in shadow or in full light, reflecting other colours from their surroundings. Also they are not always a perfect shape or in perfect condition, having maybe suffered damage from such things as frost or insects.

8 Using the blunt end of a cocktail stick (toothpick), take off the paint where the veins go. Wipe the cocktail stick (toothpick) clean each time you mark in a vein. Take note of whether the smaller veins join the centre vein all the way down, or whether they all come from the centre at the base (see Marking the veins). With many leaves, such as holly or cotoneaster, it is only necessary to put in the main vein. Note that the under side of the leaf is often a very different shade from the top surface.

9 To make variegated leaves, make them in cream paste. Cut out the shape, mark the main veins and allow to dry. Mix up white dusting powder with colourless alcohol, such as kirsch, then add a tiny amount of liquid blue and some liquid green to form a light green. Wet a small piece of natural sponge, then dip it into the light green colour. Press lightly onto the cream leaves. Allow to dry, then paint on a small area in the middle with a darker green.

Overleaf you will find templates for all the most commonly used leaves. Trace the shape onto a thin piece of cardboard and cut out with scissors. You can then use the leaf template over and over again.

Various Leaf Templates

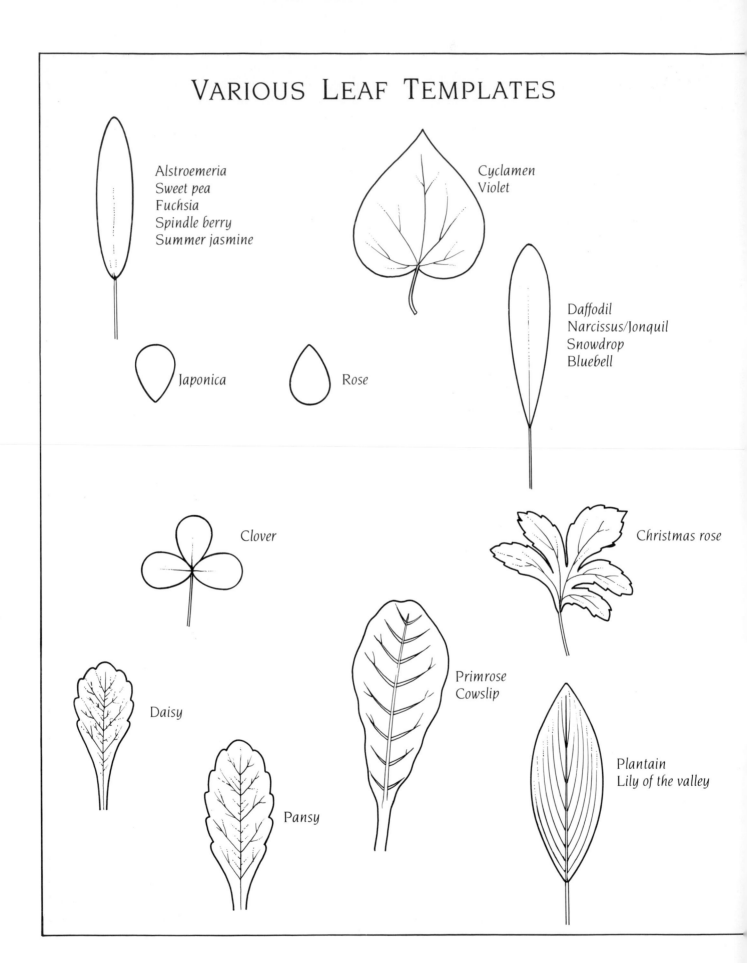

Alstroemeria
Sweet pea
Fuchsia
Spindle berry
Summer jasmine

Cyclamen
Violet

Japonica

Rose

Daffodil
Narcissus/Jonquil
Snowdrop
Bluebell

Clover

Christmas rose

Primrose
Cowslip

Daisy

Pansy

Plantain
Lily of the valley

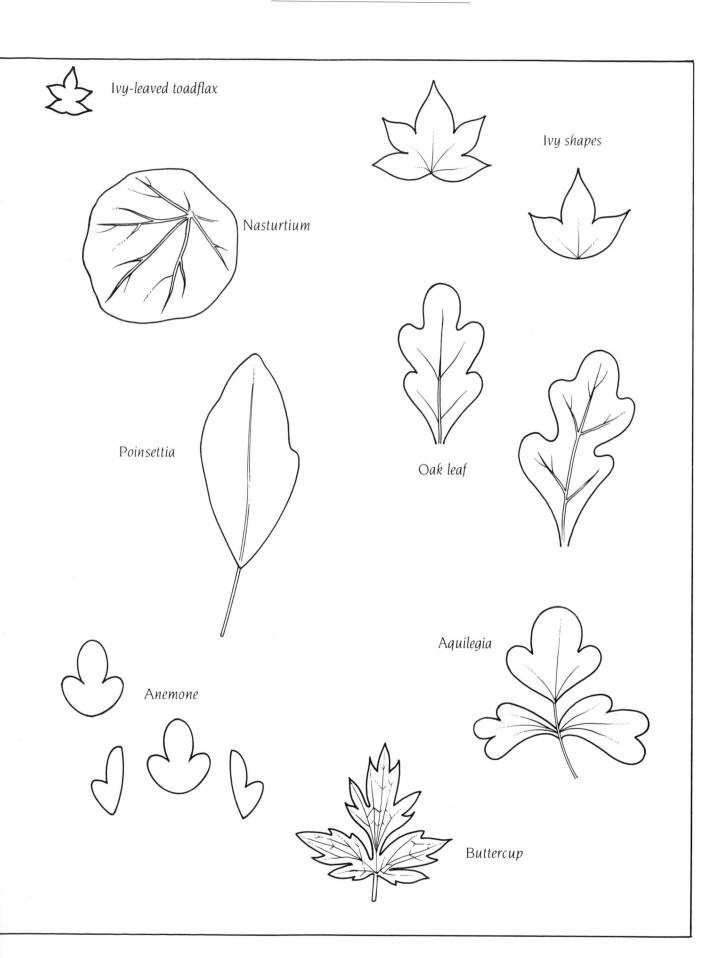

Ivy-leaved toadflax

Ivy shapes

Nasturtium

Poinsettia

Oak leaf

Aquilegia

Anemone

Buttercup

BASIC RECIPES

MAKING THE CAKE

The cakes decorated with flowers in this book are all celebration cakes – the sort you would make for a wedding, birthday, anniversary or other special occasion, so they are all made from a rich fruit cake mixture. This type of cake improves with keeping, so the cake should be made at least 2 months in advance. Alternatively, the cakes can be made with a pound cake mixture (see pages 106 and 107).

The size of cake you make will depend on the number of people you want it to serve. The charts below and on pages 106 and 107 give you a guide to quantities of ingredients and cooking times for the different size rich fruit cake tins (pans) and also for the pound cake mixture, so that you can use whatever size tin is most convenient to make either of these cakes.

The cake can then be covered with almond paste and, when that has dried, with sugarpaste. Before you can cover it with almond paste, you must prepare the cake and make an apricot glaze to stick the paste onto the cake. If the top of the cake has peaked slightly, cut it level and then turn the cake over so that the flat bottom becomes the top to which you apply the almond paste.

QUANTITIES AND TIMING FOR DIFFERENT SIZE FRUIT CAKES

TIN SIZES	18 cm (7 in) round 15 cm (6 in) square	20 cm (8 in) round 18 cm (7 in) square	23 cm (9 in) round 20 cm (8 in) square
INGREDIENTS			
plain (all-purpose) flour	250 g (8 oz/2 cups)	375 g (12 oz/3 cups)	440 g (14 oz/3 1/2 cups)
salt	pinch	pinch	pinch
mixed spice	1/2 teaspoon	1 teaspoon	1 1/2 teaspoons
cinnamon	1/2 teaspoon	1/2 teaspoon	1 teaspoon
glacé (candied) cherries	90 g (3 oz/1/2 cup)	155 g (5 oz/3/4 cup)	185 g (6 oz/1 cup)
chopped mixed peel	90 g (3 oz/1/2 cup)	125 g (4 oz/3/4 cup)	155 g (5 oz/1 cup)
butter	250 g (8 oz)	375 g (12 oz)	440 g (14 oz)
soft brown sugar	250 g (8 oz/1 1/2 cups)	375 g (12 oz/2 cups)	440 g (14 oz/2 1/3 cups)
large eggs	3	5	6
black treacle	1 tablespoon	1 1/2 tablespoons	2 tablespoons
lemons	1/2	1 small	1
oranges	1/2	1 small	1
currants	375 g (12 oz/2 1/4 cups)	500 g (1 lb/3 1/3 cups)	685 g (1 lb 6 oz/4 2/3 cups)
sultanas	220 g (7 oz/1 1/4 cups)	315 g (10 oz/1 2/3 cups)	375 g (12 oz/2 cups)
raisins	220 g (7 oz/1 1/3 cups)	315 g (10 oz/1 2/3 cups)	375 g (12 oz/2 cups)
almonds	90 g (3 oz/1/2 cup)	125 g (4 oz/3/4 cup)	155 g (5 oz/1 cup)
brandy or rum	1 tablespoon	1 1/2 tablespoons	2 tablespoons
OVEN TEMPERATURE	150C (300F/Gas 2)	150C (300F/Gas 2)	150C (300F/Gas 2)
COOKING TIME	3 hours	3 1/2 hours	4 hours

Rich Fruit Cake

750 g (1½ lb/6 cups) plain (all-purpose) flour
Large pinch salt
2 teaspoons mixed spice
2 teaspoons ground cinnamon
250 g (8 oz/1⅓ cups) glacé (candied) cherries
250 g (8 oz/1½ cups) chopped mixed peel
750 g (1½ lb) butter
750 g (1½ lb/4½ cups) soft brown sugar
11 large eggs
3 tablespoons black treacle
Finely grated zest and juice of 2 lemons
Finely grated zest and juice of 2 oranges
1.25 kg (2½ lb/7½ cups) currants
500 g (1 lb/3 cups) sultanas
500 g (1 lb/3 cups) raisins
250 g (8 oz/1½ cups) almonds, blanched and chopped
3 tablespoons brandy or rum

28 cm (11 in) round 25 cm (10 in) square	30 cm (12 in) round 28 cm (11 in) square
750 g (1½ lb/6 cups)	1.1 kg (2 lb 3 oz/8¾ cups)
pinch	large pinch
2 teaspoons	2½ teaspoons
2 teaspoons	2½ teaspoons
250 g (8 oz/1⅓ cups)	440 g (14 oz/2½ cups)
250 g (8 oz/1½ cups)	375 g (12 oz/2¼ cups)
875 g (1¾ lb)	1.1 kg (2 lb 3 oz)
875 g (1¾ lb/5¼ cups)	1.1 kg (2 lb 3 oz/6½ cups)
11	17
3 tablespoons	4 tablespoons
2	3
2	3
1.25 kg (2½ lb/7½ cups)	1.85 kg (3¾ lb/11¼ cups)
500 g (1 lb/3 cups)	815 g (1 lb 10 oz/5 cups)
500 g (1 lb/3 cups)	815 g (1 lb 10 oz/5 cups)
250 g (8 oz/1½ cups)	375 g (12 oz/2½ cups)
3 tablespoons	6 tablespoons
150C (300F/Gas 2)	150C (300F/Gas 2)
5 hours, then reduce the temperature to 130C (250F/Gas ½) for 2 hours	5½ hours, then reduce the temperature to 130C (250F/Gas ½) for 2½ hours

1 Line a 25 cm (10 in) square or a 28 cm (11 in) round cake tin (pan) with a double thickness of greased greaseproof paper. Heat the oven to 150C (300F/Gas 2).

2 In a bowl, sift together the flour, salt and spices. Wash and dry the cherries. Cut them into quarters. Wash and dry the peel.

3 Cream the butter and sugar together in a bowl until the mixture is light and fluffy. In a separate bowl, beat together the eggs, black treacle and fruit juices. Gradually beat the egg mixture into the creamed mixture. Add a little flour with the last additions of egg.

4 With a metal spoon, fold in the remaining flour, fruit zests, dried fruits and nuts. Add the brandy or rum. Fold in until the mixture has a dropping consistency. Spoon the mixture into the prepared tin (pan), spreading it out evenly into the corners, then make a small hollow in the centre.

5 Tie a double thickness of thick brown paper around the outside of the tin (pan) so that it is about 4cm (1½in) above the rim of the tin (pan). Place the tin (pan) on a pad of brown paper or newspaper on the lowest shelf in the oven. Bake for 5 hours, then lower the heat to 130C (250F/Gas ½) and cook for a further 2 hours. If the cake starts to brown too quickly, cover with greaseproof paper and then remove it about 1 hour before the end of the cooking time. If using a gas or electric oven, place a baking dish of warm water in the bottom of the oven for the duration of the baking time.

6 When a skewer inserted in the centre of the cake comes out clean or there is no sound of bubbling, the cake is cooked. Allow to stand in the tin for about 30 minutes, then turn out onto a wire tray. Leave until cold, then remove the greaseproof lining paper.

7 Wrap in a double thickness of greaseproof paper, then in foil and keep in a cool, dry, dark place for 2-3 months. During storage the cake can be enriched with additional alcohol, such as brandy, sherry or rum. To do this, unwrap and prick the surface all over with a skewer and trickle a little of the brandy, sherry or rum over the top. Wrap the cake again.

QUANTITIES AND TIMING FOR DIFFERENT SIZE POUND CAKES

TIN SIZES	18 cm (7 in) round 15 cm (6 in) square	20 cm (8 in) round 18 cm (7 in) square	23 cm (9 in) round 20 cm (8 in) square
INGREDIENTS			
eggs	5	7	8
caster sugar	250 g (8 oz/1 cup)	250 g (8 oz/1 cup)	375 g (12 oz/1½ cups)
butter	250 g (8 oz)	375 g (12 oz)	400 g (14 oz)
orange zest	from ½ orange	from ½ orange	from 1 orange
vanilla essence	½ teaspoon	1 teaspoon	1½ teaspoons
plain (all-purpose) flour	250 g (8 oz/2 cups)	375 g (12 oz/3 cups)	400 g (14 oz/3½ cups)
baking powder	½ teaspoon	½ teaspoon	1 teaspoon
salt	¼ teaspoon	¼ teaspoon	½ teaspoon
OVEN TEMPERATURE	190C (375F/Gas 5)	190C (375F/Gas 5)	190C (375F/Gas 5)
COOKING TIME	1 hour	1 hour	1 hour
SLICES	about 16	about 20	about 24

Pound Cake

---

9 eggs, separated
500 g (1 lb/2 cups) caster sugar
500 g (1 lb) butter, melted
Finely grated zest of 1 orange
2 teaspoons vanilla essence
500 g (1lb/4 cups) plain (all-purpose) flour
1 teaspoon baking powder
½ teaspoon salt

---

1 Heat the oven to 190C (375F/Gas 5). Line a greased 25 cm (10 in) square or a 28 cm (11 in) round cake tin (pan) with greased greaseproof paper.

2 Place the egg whites in a large bowl and whisk until stiff. Gradually whisk in half of the sugar until glossy.

3 Place the egg yolks and remaining sugar in a large bowl with the finely grated orange zest and the vanilla essence. Whisk until the mixture is thick and pale.

4 Sift the flour, baking powder and salt into the egg yolk mixture a quarter at a time, alternating with a quarter of the melted butter and fold in. Repeat until all the butter and flour have been folded in.

5 Fold in the whisked egg white mixture. Transfer to prepared tin (pan) and smooth the surface. Place in the preheated oven and bake for 1-1¼ hours, covering with a piece of greaseproof paper towards the end of cooking if cake becomes too brown. Insert a skewer into the cake to test if it is cooked, it should come out clean when the cake is cooked.

6 Turn the cake out onto a wire rack and peel away the paper. Leave to cool completely. Cut away a peaked top and turn over to achieve a flat top ready for icing.

POUND CAKE VARIATIONS

For the following variations – fold in the additional ingredients at stage 4 of the recipe, after the flour and butter have been incorporated.

For a 25 cm (10 in) square or 28cm (11 in) round tin (pan) add 90 g (3 oz) of any of the following: orange peel, lemon peel, sultanas, currants, raisins, glacé (candied) fruits, chopped, nuts, chopped, dried dates, chopped, dried apricots, chopped, stem ginger, chopped
125 g (4 oz/⅔ cup) of glacé (candied) cherries
1 teaspoon of almond essence
50 g (2 oz) of chocolate chips
4 tablespoons of coffee essence

28 cm (11 in) round
25 cm (10 in) square

9
500 g (1 lb/2 cups)
500 g (1 lb)
from 1 orange
2 teaspoons
500 g (1 lb/4 cups)
1 teaspoon
½ teaspoon

190C (375F/Gas 5)

1-1¼ hours

about 30

For a 20 cm (8 in) square/23 cm (9 in) round tin (pan) add 50 g (2 oz) of any of the following: orange peel, lemon peel, sultanas, currants, raisins, glacé (candied) fruits, chopped, nuts, chopped, dried dates, chopped, dried apricots, chopped, stem ginger, chopped
90 g (3 oz/½ cup) of glacé (candied) cherries
¾ teaspoon of almond essence
45 g (1½ oz) of chocolate chips
3 tablespoons of coffee essence

For a 18 cm (7 in) square/20 cm (8 in) round tin (pan) add 45 g (1½ oz) of any of the following: orange peel, lemon peel, sultanas, currants, raisins, glacé (candied) fruits, chopped, nuts, chopped, dried dates, chopped, dried apricots, chopped, stem ginger, chopped
60 g (2 oz/⅓ cup) of glacé (candied) cherries
½ teaspoon of almond essence
30 g (1 oz) of chocolate chips
2 tablespoons of coffee essence

For a 15 cm (6 in) square/18 cm (7 in) round tin (pan) add 30 g (1 oz) of any of the following: orange peel, lemon peel, sultanas, currants, raisins, glacé (candied) fruits, chopped, nuts, chopped, dried dates, chopped, dried apricots, chopped, stem ginger, chopped
30 g (1 oz/2 tablespoons) of glacé (candied) cherries
½ teaspoon of almond essence
30 g (1 oz) of chocolate chips
1 tablespoon of coffee essence

MAKING SHAPED CAKES

A fancy-shaped cake tin (pan) will automatically give you a decorative shape. Heart-shaped and numeral tins are available from large stores. However, if you do not want the expense of a special tin (pan), a knife can easily be used to produce beautiful decorative cakes starting with a plain square or round shape – choose your design according to the cake tins you own. The simplest shape to cut from a square is an octagon and from a round cake is a heart, but a star or horseshoe can also be cut from a round cake quite easily, using a template to help you cut the decorative shape more accurately.

To make a shaped cake like the Cyclamen cake or Snowdrop cake (see pages 83 and 91), bake the cake in a round tin (pan), then make a template of the design you want. First trace your design onto a piece of lightweight cardboard. This should correspond exactly with the dimensions of the cake tin, so that the minimum amount of cake is cut away for the design.

Put the cake on a board and place the cardboard template on top of the cake, then cut round it to cut the cake to the same shape. Hold the knife vertically at the side of the template and use a sawing motion to cut as this gives an even, neat cake edge.

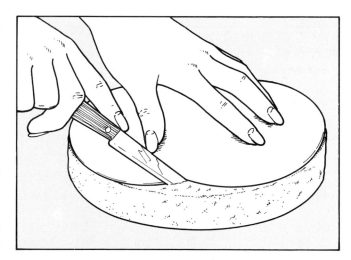

Cutting the shape: place the cardboard template on top of the cake, then cut round it to cut the cake to the same shape. Hold the knife vertically at the side of the template and use a sawing motion to cut as this gives an even, neat cake edge.

Apricot Glaze

This glaze is used to make the almond paste stick securely to the cake.

---

3 tablespoons apricot jam
Squeeze of lemon juice

---

1 Sieve the jam into a small, heavy-based saucepan. Add the lemon juice and melt over a low heat. Brush onto the cake.

2 The fruit cakes in this book are covered with bought almond paste as this is made with pasteurised egg. To cover the cake with almond paste, first weigh the cake, then take half this measurement i.e. for a 2.5 kg (5 lb) cake 1.25 kg (2½ lb) almond paste.

3 Roll out almond paste to a thickness of 5 mm (¼ in) thick. Pick up almond paste by gently pulling it over the rolling pin (like pastry) and place straight over the cake. For larger cakes – 25 cm (10 in) upwards – get your hands well underneath and gently but quickly pick up almond paste and place right over the cake.

QUANTITIES OF ALMOND PASTE

	TIN SIZE			
ROUND	15 cm	18 cm	20 cm	23 cm
	(6 in)	(7 in)	(8 in)	(9 in)
SQUARE		15 cm	18 cm	20 cm
		(6 in)	(7 in)	(8 in)
ALMOND PASTE	375 g	500 g	625 g	875 g
	(12 oz)	(1 lb)	(1¼ lb)	(1¾ lb)
	TIN SIZE			
ROUND	25 cm	28 cm	30 cm	
	(10 in)	(11 in)	(12 in)	
SQUARE	23 cm	25 cm	28 cm	30 cm
	(9 in)	(10 in)	(11 in)	(12 in)
ALMOND PASTE	1 kg	1.1 kg	1.25 kg	1.5 kg
	(2 lb)	(2¼ lb)	(2½ lb)	(3 lb)

Royal icing

Although all the cakes are covered with sugarpaste, you will need royal icing for some of the decorative work on cakes such as the Thistle cake (see page 94).

---

1 egg white
250 g (8 oz/1½ cups) icing (confectioners') sugar, sifted
1 tablespoon lemon juice

---

1 Put the egg white in a bowl and beat with an electric or rotary beater until it is frothy. Stir in the sugar with a wooden spoon, 1 tablespoon at a time. Beat well after each addition to make sure the sugar is incorporated into the egg white before adding any more.

2 When half the sugar has been added, stir in the lemon juice with a wooden spoon, then beat in the remaining sugar. Beat until the icing forms soft peaks when you lift up the beater. Cover with a damp cloth and leave for 2-3 hours.

Royal icing lacework

To make the lacework shown on the Thistle and other cakes, put the icing in a piping (pastry) bag fitted with a size 0 plain writing tube (nozzle). Split open a plastic roasting bag. Place a piece of graph paper divided into 2 cm (¾ in) squares on a board and place the plastic roasting bag over it; secure with masking tape. Pipe the pattern shown on the right in each square. The dots are then piped where the weak points occur.

To position the individual pieces of royal icing lacework on the side of a cake, mark the sugarpaste covering on the cake where you want the lacework to be positioned i.e. either in a straight line or in a curve (use the shaper template opposite to mark the shape of a curve). Then pipe seven dots at a time close together (the width of one of the laceworks) and fix one of the laceworks onto the dots.

Pipe another seven dots next to the first ones and fix on the next lacework. Continue round the cake, leaving gaps if you want to position flowers or any other decorations on the cake board at the side of the cake.

SHAPER TEMPLATES

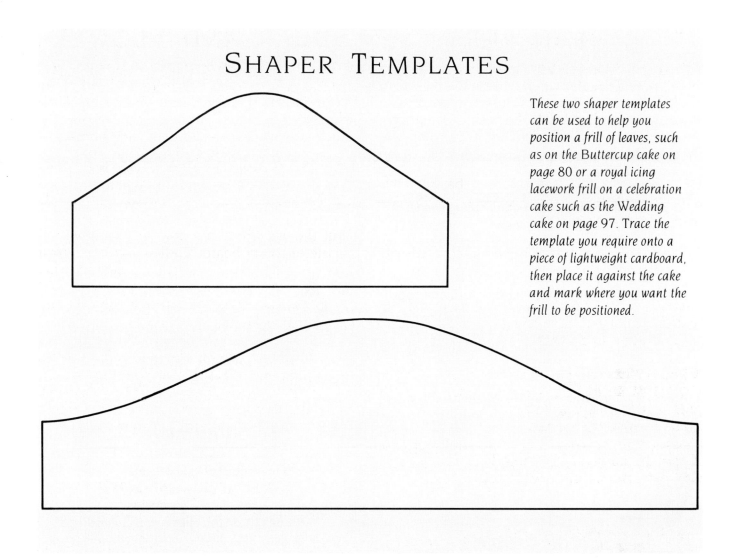

These two shaper templates can be used to help you position a frill of leaves, such as on the Buttercup cake on page 80 or a royal icing lacework frill on a celebration cake such as the Wedding cake on page 97. Trace the template you require onto a piece of lightweight cardboard, then place it against the cake and mark where you want the frill to be positioned.

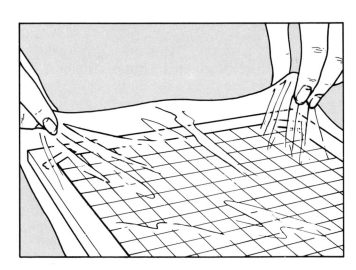

Covering the graph paper: *split open a plastic roasting bag. Place a piece of graph paper divided into 2 cm (¾ in) squares on a board and place the plastic roasting bag over it. Secure the plastic with masking tape so that it is quite smooth.*

Piping the lacework pattern: *put some royal icing in a piping (pastry) bag fitted with a size 0 plain writing tube (nozzle) and pipe the pattern shown above onto the plastic in each square. Dots are piped where the weak points occur.*

Gum arabic solution

If you do not want to use egg white for painting on the petals or calyx when making the flowers in this book, you can use this solution instead. Gum arabic solution can be mixed with different coloured concentrated liquid colourings when you are painting leaves and will give more body to the colour you are using.

---

3 parts boiled water, rose water or orange water
1 part gum arabic

---

1 Sterilise a heatproof bowl, saucepan, sieve and suitable container for putting the gum arabic solution in by rinsing thoroughly with boiling water. Put the water, rose water or orange water into a heatproof bowl and sprinkle the gum arabic on top of the liquid.

2 Place the container in a saucepan of warm water and heat gently until the gum arabic has dissolved. Strain the gum arabic solution through the sterilised sieve into the prepared container; the solution is now ready to use.

Gelatine droplets

These tiny, clear droplets of gelatine look like raindrops when they are used as part of the decoration on cakes like the Buttercup cake (see page 80).

---

2 tablespoons cold water
2 teaspoons powdered gelatine

---

1 Put the water in a small heatproof bowl, sprinkle over the gelatine and leave to soften for 2-3 minutes. Stand the bowl in a saucepan of hot water and heat very gently, stirring, until the gelatine has completely dissolved.

2 Stretch some plastic roasting wrap over a board. Suck up the dissolved gelatine in a dropper, then dot it over the plastic wrap a drop at a time. Leave to dry before sticking onto leaves with a tiny amount of royal icing.

SUGAR AND FLOWER PASTES

All the cakes in this book are covered with sugarpaste, which is rolled out and moulded over the cake. It is also known as fondant icing but should not be confused with pouring fondant, or decorating icing. Sugarpaste can be bought in ready-to-use blocks, but is quite straight-forward to make.

The flowers are made with flower or modelling paste, a sweet paste that is made with sugar but is firmer than sugarpaste and easier to model. Three different recipes for flower paste are given here; which paste you use to make the flowers is largely a matter of personal choice. Individual skin type affects the paste – some people require a paste with more fat, others less fat or more cornflour (cornstarch) for example. Experiment until you find the one that suits you best.

Sugarpaste

---

5 teaspoons powdered gelatine
50 ml (2 fl oz/¼ cup) water
3 teaspoons glycerine
125 ml (4 fl oz/1½ cup) liquid glucose
900 g (1 lb 13 oz/5½ cups) icing (confectioners') sugar
Food colouring (optional)
Kirsh, for brushing
Extra icing (confectioners') sugar and cornflour (cornstarch), for dusting

---

1 Sprinkle the gelatine over the water in a small heatproof bowl and leave to soften for 2-3 minutes. Stand the bowl in a saucepan of hot water and heat gently, stirring, until dissolved and quite hot. Stir in the glycerine and glucose.

2 Sift the icing (confectioners') sugar into a bowl. Make a well in centre and pour in gelatine mixture. Mix, then knead until paste is a soft consistency. Work in food colouring, if using. Brush a little kirsh over the almond paste.

3 Sift a little icing (confectioners') sugar over a work surface and roll out the sugarpaste. Cover the cake as for almond paste (see page 108).

4 Dust your hands with cornflour (cornstarch) and rotate the palm of your hand on the top of the cake to smooth the paste and expel any air. Gently smooth the sides to the shape of the cake. Trim the paste at the base of the cake, if necessary. Smooth the surface of the paste with a cake smoother to remove any creases, tiny holes and other blemishes in it.

Flower paste

---

250 g (8 oz/1 ½ cups) icing (confectioners') sugar
2 teaspoons powdered gelatine
6 teaspoons water
1 rounded teaspoon glucose

---

1 Sift the icing (confectioners') sugar into a bowl. Sprinkle the gelatine over the water in a small heat-proof bowl and leave to soften for 2-3 minutes. Stand the bowl in a saucepan of hot water and heat gently, stirring, until dissolved and quite hot. Add the glucose. The liquid should be quite clear before adding to the icing (confectioners') sugar.

2 Make a well in the centre of the icing (confectioners') sugar and stir in the gelatine mixture with a knife to make a firm paste. Place the paste in a plastic bag inside an airtight container. Leave to stand at room temperature for 3-4 hours before using to make the flowers and leaves.

Flower paste made in a mixer

---

500 g (1 lb/3 cups) icing (confectioners') sugar
3 teaspoons gum tragacanth
2 teaspoons powdered gelatine
5 teaspoons warm water
2 teaspoons liquid glucose
10 g (⅓ oz) white vegetable fat (shortening) or
2 teaspoons soya oil
1 large egg white

---

1 Sift icing (confectioners') sugar into a bowl and mix in the gum tragacanth. Warm in the oven, over a pan of hot water, or in the microwave (you can use the mixer bowl if heating over hot water or in the microwave). Meanwhile, put all the remaining ingredients except the egg white into a bowl over a pan of hot water and heat until liquid. Pour the liquid into the warm sugar.

2 Warm the mixer beater. Transfer the sugar mixture to the mixer bowl if not already in it. With the mixer at its lowest speed, pour in the egg white, placing a cloth over the top as the mixture starts to take up the egg white. Beat until the mixture begins to cool; as it thickens it will come away from the side of the bowl in strings. Store the paste in a plastic bag in an airtight container in the refrigerator. Leave for 24 hours before using.

Flower paste made in the microwave

---

315 g (10 oz/2 cups) icing (confectioners') sugar, sifted
3 times
4½ teaspoons gum tragacanth
1 heaped plus 1 almost level teaspoon powdered gelatine
5 teaspoons water
1 extra large egg white, thread removed

---

1 Grease mixing bowl with white fat (shortening). Put half the icing (confectioners') sugar in the bowl and stir in the gum tragacanth. Sprinkle the gelatine onto the water in a small bowl or cup; set aside while microwaving the icing (confectioners') sugar and gum tragacanth.

2 Microwave the icing (confectioners') sugar on HIGH for 50 seconds and then stir. Repeat the microwaving and stirring twice more. Microwave the gelatine on HIGH for 16 seconds.

3 Pour the gelatine into the warm icing (confectioners') sugar and beat just a little. Stir the egg white slightly, then beat vigorously into the sugar mixture (it is very important to beat very thoroughly and quickly), until the mixture is creamy white and fluffy. Beat in the remaining icing (confectioners') sugar.

4 Knead the paste thoroughly, then place in a plastic bag inside an airtight container. Leave in the refrigerator for 24 hours before using. The paste is very soft after mixing but is fairly stiff after 24 hours in the refrigerator. A little extra egg white can be kneaded into the paste at this stage if necessary.

INDEX